# The Khmer Empire

*A Captivating Guide to the Merged Kingdoms of Cambodia That Became the Angkor Empire That Ruled over Most of Mainland Southeast Asia and Parts of Southern China*

# Free Bonus from Captivating History (Available for a Limited time)

Hi History Lovers!

Now you have a chance to join our exclusive history list so you can get your first history ebook for free as well as discounts and a potential to get more history books for free! Simply visit the link below to join.

Captivatinghistory.com/ebook

Also, make sure to follow us on Facebook, Twitter and Youtube by searching for Captivating History.

# Contents

# Introduction

The image of Angkor Wat, one of the greatest temples in the world, decorates the national flag of modern-day Cambodia. Cambodia is the only country in the world that has an image of ruins on its national flag, but such a thing comes naturally to this Southeast Asian country. Angkor is their heritage, their birthright, and a crucial component of their national identity. Between the $10^{th}$ and $15^{th}$ centuries, Angkor was the center of the Khmer Empire. It is a name of a city, a region, and the whole kingdom that once dominated the political, cultural, and economic world of Southeast Asia. The name of the capital at the time was Yasodharapura, named after its founder Yasovarman I. At its economic and social peak, the city housed over a million people, and at the time, it was one of the most densely populated cities in the world. The riches of this city and its ruler came from the understanding that manpower was more valuable than gold.

However, what we know of the Khmer civilization and Yasodharapura comes from its streets, water systems, reservoirs, and, most importantly, temples. No ordinary houses, not even the royal palace, survived the tooth of time. After all, the human habitats of all social ranks were built out of perishable materials. Only the gods and their houses were worthy enough to be built out of stone. The water systems, reservoirs, and streets were given religious meaning;

therefore, they too deserved the strong and sturdy materials that can resist time. Although kings and their immediate family were depicted in stone, they were given the image of the divine. The Khmer kings are depicted in the images of Shiva, Vishnu, and later Buddha, and their ancestors were depicted as the various aspects of the divine. The crown jewel of the Empire of Angkor was its temple, Angkor Wat.

Angkor Wat, which was built in the 12<sup>th</sup> century as the monument to King Suryavarman II and also served as his tomb, breaks the tradition of Hindu Shaivism. It was almost as if the temple was built in a different order and with a different organization and orientation, as it breaks all the rules of the Khmer culture. Or at least so it seemed to the unwise eye of the Western scholars who tried to unravel its mysteries. Angkor Wat stands witness to the new religious ideology of the Khmer civilization, for it is a symbol of Vaishnavism. It seems as if Suryavarman II's reign came as a turning point for the whole Khmer Empire.

The Khmer Empire, also known as the Empire of Angkor, wasn't an empire in the modern sense of the word. It can hardly be called a kingdom in Western views. It is a designation given to the Khmer civilization that prospered between the 10<sup>th</sup> and 15<sup>th</sup> centuries to differentiate it from other periods of Cambodian history. Nevertheless, the Khmer Empire was a complex civilization, with the kings at the very top of society. The people warred with the neighboring tribes, worked their land and grew rice, and were builders responsible for one of the most elaborate complexes of temples and monuments in the world. The Khmer Empire was a nation of slaves and rulers, of Hinduism and Buddhism, of tradition and innovative engineering—truly, the Khmer people of the Empire of Angkor were a paradoxical entity.

The late 12<sup>th</sup> and early 13<sup>th</sup> centuries saw the reign of Jayavarman VI, one of the most renowned kings of the Khmer Empire. He rebuilt the walls of Yasodharapura and founded its new center, with his Bayon Temple in the middle. He battled with the neighboring kingdoms and expanded the territory of Angkor, but after his death, the kingdom started its long and continuous downfall. Many incompetent rulers, internal succession struggles, and foreign invasions took turns inflicting damage on the Khmer, and they each influenced the destiny of this great civilization. By the 15<sup>th</sup> century, Angkor was abandoned, and a new capital was founded in Phnom Penh (where it still stands). But Angkor was never really deserted. People continued to find shelter among the walls and ruins, whether it be from wars or from natural disasters. The jungle enveloped Angkor Wat as if to protect its beauty from the desolation of time and war that raged outside its walls, only to reveal it when the people were ready to respect the works of their ancestors once more.

When Cambodia became a French protectorate, the jungle was cut down, and the ruins of the Khmer Empire saw the light of day again. The patient work of Khmer and French archaeologists brought the ruins back to life, and Angkor Wat is one of the most visited monuments in the world today, counting over 2.6 million people each year. The site is still enveloped in mysticism and spirituality, which only makes it more attractive and magical. It is no wonder people rush to sit on the stone walls and observe the glorious sunset over the lotus bud-shaped rooftops of ancient temples. It is a sight to marvel and pay honor to the glorious past of the Khmer people.

# Chapter 1 – The Foundations of the Khmer Empire

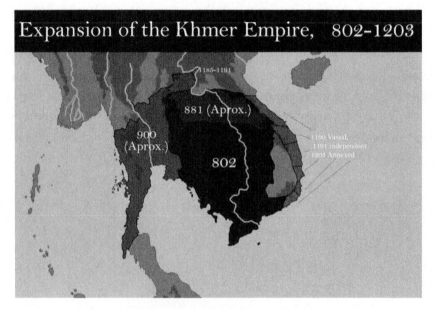

The expansion of the Khmer Empire

The history of the Khmer Empire, which lasted from the 9<sup>th</sup> to the 15<sup>th</sup> century, is but a fragment of Cambodian history. The empire always referred to itself as Kambujadesa (or Kambuja), signaling it belongs to a wider historical narrative. The term Khmer Empire, or Empire of Angkor, is used today by scholars to mark the period of history in which the empire rose to power. Khmer is a name for the people of Cambodia, and even today, they represent over 90 percent of the overall population. They speak the Khmer language and are native to the South Asian mainland. Khmer people have their own origin myth that says how a Hindu Brahmin married an apsara, a celestial spirit named Mera. Out of their union, the Khmer people came to be. In the light of modern history, this myth might be a depiction of the Indianization of the native Khmer population. However, today's scholars cannot pinpoint the origins of the Khmer, and the most vocalized belief is that they are a mixture of different people of Southeast Asia, notably the Chinese and the Indus.

The history of the Khmer Empire lacks sources, and anything we know about its existence comes from the sparse stone carvings, archaeological work, and written testimonials of the Chinese diplomats and merchants. Although the 9<sup>th</sup> century is regarded as the beginning of the Khmer Empire, it is important to know the political and cultural scene of the Cambodian territories out of which the empire rose. The first document dated to the early history of Cambodia is from the 7<sup>th</sup> century, and it is written in the Khmer language. There are around two hundred such documents, some written in Khmer, others in Sanskrit. When put together, these documents give us an incomplete but realistic picture of Cambodian society of the period. The inscriptions written in Sanskrit were all written in verse, and they praised the deeds of gods and kings. The Khmer language was reserved for the documents that dealt with the common people, who were ruled by these gods and kings. This creates the image of a society divided into two parts: those who spoke and understood only the Khmer language and those who were able to write and read Sanskrit. The Sanskrit inscriptions mainly talk about the kings who built Hindu and Buddhist monasteries and temples, the generous donations to the monasteries, and the victories in wars. Brahmins are also praised, as they were above any other social class. The Sanskrit texts are comparable to the verses written in India at the time, but the Cambodians preferred subtle words and slightly different compositions of the poetry.

Khmer inscriptions are written only in prose. They are texts that describe the founding of temples and their administration. They are the lists of people's names who are attached to the founding of certain temples and lists of a temple's inventory. They also describe the land, orchards, and rice fields in the temple's jurisdiction by listing their dimensions. From these texts, we can also learn what the duties of slaves and the amount of taxes the temples gathered were. They could be either paid in labor or in kind. These texts usually end in a curse that was supposed to threaten those who refused to abide by the temple's rules.

This division of the ancient Khmer people into two languages demonstrates the division between the rich and poor, the elite and the commoners. The elite layer of society contained the royal family and the priests. They were protected by the gods since they had direct access to them. They cherished poetry, art, intricacy, wordplay, and wealth. On the other hand, the Khmer-speaking layer of society was poor, wrote only in prose, and kept straightforward catalogs of ordinary, earthly people and possessions. These documents, both Khmer and Sanskrit, were carved in stone, usually on temple doors and columns or freestanding steles. Scholars presume these documents were also written on some kind of perishable material and were archived inside the temples, but the traces of these have not yet been found.

The duality between the languages, the social classes, and the writing material is also displayed in the use of stone. The texts were carved into stone because it was considered a divine material; thus, it was reserved only for the divine. That is why the secular buildings were never built out of stone, only the temples. Commoner's houses, dwellings of the Brahmins, and even the palace were built out of perishable materials such as wood and bamboo. The early Khmer society made a distinct difference between the earthly, perishable, and human, and the celestial, permanent, and divine. Many curses and oaths of loyalty were found inscribed on stone, presumably to make them permanent and stronger.

Aside from the social division between the elite and the commoners, there was a third group of people, but they made up only around 10 percent of society. They were the artists, clerks, concubines, artisans, high officials, and priests. During the Angkorian period, they were divided into castes or *varna*, depending on their occupation. They never served as slaves, but they were also very rarely patrons of the temples. Because of this, their names are not inscribed in stone and are forever lost. Today, we cannot know who were the artists and artisans behind the building of the great temples of Cambodia. The poor people worked the rice fields, and their only ambition was to become one of the privileged caste groups so they could get out of the muddy fields.

It is hard to translate the ancient Cambodian social terms, as their meaning is incomprehensible by Western standards. To Western society, the term "king" usually bears the connotation of medieval European kings. But in early Cambodian society, the king, or raja as they called him, has a different meaning. The raja was a ruler, but he was not what Westerners consider a king. It is a similar case for the term for slaves. In the Khmer language, this term is *knjom*, and a person designated with it had more rights than slaves of Western civilizations. But pre-Angkorian Cambodia had fourteen different categories of slaves, and it is impossible to understand them all when looked through the prism of the Western world. The slaves in old Cambodia were divided into different categories based on their origin, their social status, and the duties they performed. Perhaps the field laborers are the slave class that comes closest to the Western understanding of the term. But others, especially those attached to the temples, had different kinds of freedoms and limitations. They might have even been considered quasi-clerics. But what separated them from the free people was the fact that they could be sold and bought. They were not servants either, as they had no right to leave their service when and if they wished. If they tried to run away, they were punished.

Many of the slaves were bondsmen who worked their debt away. Some of them were even sold by their parents, and instances of hereditary servitude have been recorded. Because the slaves rarely moved and were completely attached to the territory they served in, it is possible they were never strictly attached to their owner. Generations of slaves of the same family could serve in the same territory but under different lords, but this was not always the case. Some slaves were owned by temples and by the elite members of society and were attached to their owners rather than the territory. However, it is difficult to generalize Cambodian society between the 7th and 9th centuries as the evidence is lacking. The best possible guess is that the practices varied depending on the period and the territory. Names of slaves were often written down, as they were considered possessions and had to be cataloged. Some of these names were written down respectfully, and a simple Mr. or Ms. was added to their names in Sanskrit. But the use of derogatory terms was also a norm, and many slaves were simply named "dog," "red-in-face," or "bad-smelling-one." Slaves whose names were written in Sanskrit had higher status, and they usually served as entertainers, dancers, and musicians. Their names were elaborate, poetic, and even in use today in Cambodia. They ranged from "loves justice" to various names of flowers and other botanical elements.

The Cambodian communists of the 1970s tried to represent medieval Cambodian society as being feudal, but it is clear that it wasn't. Slaves represented the majority of the population, but free peasants did exist, and they inhabited villages that were allowed to grow rice. However, the peasants had to answer the call of their rulers and join the war efforts or help in building a temple or a monastery. They were obligated to perform public works, and many of the free peasants were war prisoners or their descendants. It seems that both free peasants and slaves didn't have the aspirations for freedom and richness. They shared their masters' culture and religion, and they saw the wealth of the elite as the means of their protection. They were eager to serve, as servitude meant comfort and safety. Elevation to a better social position was possible, but it was very rare, as an individual needed a special talent and distinction. That talent also had to be recognized by the Brahmins or priests, and they rarely allowed themselves to be involved with the lower classes in the first place.

Early Cambodia's economy was based on rice. The natives were growing dry rice (flooded with rains, naturally) and root vegetables even before irrigation systems and wet rice (flooded through the irrigation system, not dependent on rain) were introduced during the Hinduization of the communities. Growing rice demands people, especially wet cultivation. People are needed to work in the mud and to maintain the irrigation system. That is why the overlordship and power in Southeast Asia, in general, meant ruling the people, not the territory. Of course, the kings and chieftains needed territory to grow rice in the first place, but the majority of Cambodia was blanketed by forests anyway, and the states had to work with what little territory they had. During the Angkorian period, the Khmer Empire extended its territory but only to the territory that could be used to grow more rice. It was only during the 12$^{th}$ century that the ownership of a territory became a sign of the king's prestige. But even then, it didn't last for long, as the rulers quickly recognized that it was far more important to control the people than the land.

The king was the owner of the people and the land, which was why only the king was able to grant the land for the people to use. Many Angkorian texts deal with the complicated disputes over the land and the access to it, as well as with the labor resources needed to cultivate that land. But the whole territory of Cambodia was divided into small kingdoms, or states, that were ruled by their elite. Each state had a collection of people that worked the land and could be called upon in times of war. These kingdoms traded with each other and raided each other when they were in need of more slaves. The kings of each kingdom considered themselves universal monarchs, as they were taught by Indian teachings. But they also considered themselves local chieftains according to the Cambodian tradition, as they dealt with secular tasks of the kingdom too.

The ability to lead was measured by one's success on the battlefield and his ability to attract a large base of followers. The leader also had to demonstrate his knowledge of religious rituals, and he had to protect his people in times of need. This protection wasn't only needed during times of war. The king had to be able to protect the peasants and slaves from the natural forces, the wrath of the gods, and from rival rulers. Because of this, many rulers throughout Cambodian history added the suffix *varman* to their names. It is an old Sanskrit word for defensive armor; therefore, it means protection. But rulers themselves needed protection too, and because of their high status, that protection needed to be supernatural and divine, mainly coming from the supreme god Shiva. A king's devotion to Shiva was displayed through a series of rituals that he performed to transfer the god's potency onto his kingdom and its people. These rituals included human sacrifice and were performed at the beginning of the cultivation season. Rulers used this ritual even in the 19th century. The main goal of the rituals was to transfer divine fertility onto the rice fields and on the people.

Hinduism was the main state religion of the pre-Khmer and Khmer empires. It came to the territories of Cambodia during the Funan era, which is placed between 100 BCE and 500 CE. Even when the Funan kingdom was replaced by the Khmer Empire, Hinduism remained the main religion and Vishnu and Shiva the main deities. In the $12^{th}$ century, Angkor Wat was built, and to this day, it is the largest Hindu temple in the world. During the Funan kingdom and the Khmer Empire, Hindu temples were decorated with relief carvings of various scenes from the *Ramayana* (an ancient Indian epic, called *Reamker* in Khmer) and depictions of the Hindu deities.

During the Khmer Empire, Buddhism was also a popular religion. Two Khmer kings were even Mahayana Buddhists. Buddhism entered Cambodia during the Funan era, but it never became a dominant religion. After the Funan kingdom dissolved and was succeeded by the Chenla kingdom (500–700 CE), the number of Buddhists dropped significantly, but the religion managed to survive. The first kings of the Khmer Empire declared themselves as Hindu god-kings, but they were incredibly tolerant of Buddhism. They even financed their monasteries. Jayavarman VII (r. 1181–1215) wasn't the first Buddhist king, but he was the first to make it a state religion. From this point, Hinduism and Buddhism would rotate as the main state religions, but Hinduism often prevailed. During the rule of Indravarman II (1219–1243), Hinduism was again the main religion. This dualism of religion was also reflected in the temples and statues of the deities. Cambodia is full of beautiful old temples, which depict Buddha with Hindu elements or Vishnu and Shiva with the elements of Buddha. Whichever religion was dominant at the time, the holy sites were simply changed and decorated to serve the latest religious trend. Jayavarman VII, a Mahayana Buddhist himself, sent his son, Indravarman II, to Sri Lanka for ten years, where he studied Theravada Buddhism. Eventually, when Indravarman II took the throne, Theravada Buddhism became the dominant religion, and it is believed that many social changes occurred that helped contribute to the end of the empire. Theravada Buddhism remains the dominant religion of modern Cambodia, with over 95 percent of its citizens practicing it. However, Hindu influences can still be seen in Cambodian culture.

Aside from Hinduism and Buddhism, local belief systems were also in place. These religious cults were imported mainly from China, and they represented various forms of paying respect to one's ancestors. They were always oriented toward the community, as the benefits of a whole community prevailed over the needs of the individual. These local religions often included human sacrifice among their rituals, but they mainly targeted agricultural benefits. Some of these rituals are still practiced in rural Cambodia, but they most likely have changed over time. Royals still perform the rituals in which they talk to dead ancestors to secure welfare for the whole kingdom.

The Khmer people believe in the existence of many spirits. Their ancestor spirits are probably the most widespread belief, and they are called *Nakta*. But in old Cambodia, genealogies were not kept, so these ancestors had no names. That is why *Nakta* became the ancestor spirits of the communities in certain territories. *Nakta* had the power to bring social justice to individuals and whole communities, and they also brought security, peace, and health to the community and their descendants. Although they are the spirits of the ancestors, some *Nakta* were considered wild and unpredictable. These wild spirits usually inhabited abandoned places, and the Khmer people would avoid uninhabited settlements because they believed that wild *Nakta* were too powerful and evil. Over time and due to the synchronization of the religions, local spirits in some Khmer communities received the names of Hindu gods. The temples were built on sites that were already considered sacred by the local population. In times when the influence of Hinduism and the priests declined, the local population preyed on the statues of the gods as if they were the representations of *Nakta*.

One of the Hindu cults that received a transformation among the Khmer population was the worship of lingam, a phallus-shaped stone, which represented the sexual union of Shiva and the universe. During the Angkorian era, many lingams were carved, and when Hinduism declined, the local population continued to practice its cult because of the belief that lingams were the connection between the ancestors and the earth. Wherever lingams were built, the ground around it was considered fertile and good for starting a rice field. Lingams were sometimes ceremoniously moved from one site to another, as it was believed that they brought fertility to the new location. At the same time, it was believed that the old location would lose its fertility.

Cambodia was on the main trading route between China and India, so it is not a surprise that both Hinduism and Buddhism entered the country. These religions mixed with the local cults and created a unique culture. The country is still filled with the temples in which Shiva and Vishnu took the shape of Buddha or where Buddha is adorned with Hindu symbolic ornaments.

# Chapter 2 – The Founding of the Empire

Drawing of Jayavarman II praying to Shiva

*Khmerloy9, CC0, via Wikimedia Commons*
*https://commons.wikimedia.org/wiki/File:Chey_Varaman_Teveak_Reach.jpg*

The Angkorian era is roughly placed between 802 and 1431. But these years shouldn't be taken as the beginning and end of the Khmer Empire. The Khmer people lived in the area of Angkor for centuries before the state was even created. The city itself came into existence during the 9th century, and its name is a Sanskrit word meaning "city." The city was abandoned during the 15th century, but that wasn't a sudden occurrence, and there were people still living in Angkor at the time. It only lost its status as the royal city. But in the 1570s, the royal seat was returned to Angkor, although very briefly. The main temple of the city, Angkor Wat, was never really abandoned. It continued to operate at least until the 19th century, as newer statues of Buddha were found. The most recent scripture on the temple walls was dated to 1747. Even when the French archaeologists found Angkor Wat in the 19th century, the temple grounds were inhabited and maintained by several hundred slaves.

The dates that are usually taken as the beginning and the end of the Khmer Empire are nothing more than the representation of Cambodia's golden age. Between 802 and 1431, the Khmer Empire, or Kambujadesa, was the mightiest state in Southeast Asia. As such, it was a place often visited by many peoples. Pilgrims and merchants came from as far as Malaysia and Burma, as well as the kingdoms of the Thai territory to the west.

But even though the Khmer Empire dominated the whole region, we knew very little about it. We can only guess that some of its kings ruled as despots, while others didn't do anything for the kingdom. Some were completely forgotten, yet others left scores of temples, statues, inscriptions in stones, and public works. Even the administration seems to have changed over time. At some points, it was centralized and multileveled, but at other times, it seems as if the state had to oversee only several hundred followers. The history of the Angkorian period is very easy to generalize, but it is hard to understand on a deeper level. From the archaeological evidence, Sanskrit poems, and Chinese records, it is easy to see that Khmer prospered in some periods but declined in others. However, there is no evidence that explains why this happened. The Khmer scriptures left behind offer us glimpses into the cultural and material life of Cambodia at the time, but it is difficult to come to any conclusions when all a scholar has as evidence are lists of slaves, temple inventories, and royal possessions. Imagine if scholars had only decrees, deeds, and the emperors' wills as references to the whole history of the Roman Empire!

Luckily, the Khmer meticulously dated their inscriptions, so the chronological framework of Angkor is easy to deduce. Because of this, it was easy to reconstruct the chronological order in which the kings ruled the empire, even after the Cambodians themselves forgot. For this chronological reconstruction, the historians are thankful to French scholar George Coedès (1886–1968), who dedicated his life to the history of Southeast Asia. Coedès's magnum opus is the translation and dating of thousands of Cambodian pre-Angkorian and Angkorian inscriptions, which he published in eight tomes. But these inscriptions are not where we can get the information and details about the rural life of Cambodia or the life of the commoners in general. They cannot even teach us anything about the political system of Angkor as either the city or the empire. The documents rarely refer to any events, and even if they do, they are some of the more extraordinary events, such as the contracts between gods and the royal family written in Sanskrit poems or those among the people, which were written in Khmer prose.

The whole history of the Angkorian era can only be looked at through the cracks in the wall. Each crack gives us a glimpse into an event but not the context around it. We can say that the hypothetical "Temple X" was built on a certain date and was dedicated to this or that Indian god. We can see that it had this many slaves attached to it. The slaves were usually divided into lists by gender, and the children were listed by their ability to walk or if they were infants. We can also learn whether the temple grounds stretched to the east, approaching that hill, or to the west, where a certain stream or river was a border to its territories. But that is it. Temple X's context in the Angkorian period remains unknown. We will never learn how important it was or if its patrons were royals or Brahmins. Scripts like this are numerous in archaeological sites of the Khmer Empire, but they are often nothing more but stand-alone inscriptions on pieces of what used to be a temple's wall. These fragments of Khmer history became a part of the Cambodian landscape, with many monuments and steles scattered in uninhabited areas. As they were abandoned by their people and far away from their memory, temple grounds and monuments were taken over by nature.

Other than temple inscriptions, numerous temples around Cambodia still stand as witnesses to the Khmer Empire's history. They are filled with statues and bas-reliefs, as well as various artifacts. The temples tell us a story of the religious priorities of the royal family, about the popularity of myths and their meaning in the everyday life of Cambodians. From the statues, we can learn about the fashion trends of the time, as they are adorned with the popular hairstyles, pieces of jewelry, and hemlines of the period. The bas-reliefs often depict the armies, and from them, we can learn about the weapons the Angkorian soldiers used, their armor, and sometimes even their battle tactics. What the Angkorian-era documentation is missing is the larger context, a view of the overall society, politics, and culture of the period. The details about the taxes people paid, land ownership, stories of ordinary lives, and folklore remain a complete mystery.

### Jayavarman II (c. 770–850; r. 802–850)

Sdok Kok Thom, an 11th-century Khmer temple in what is today southeastern Thailand, was, for a long time, a source of the chronology and history of the early Angkorian era. The inscription describes the event that took place in 802 at Phnom Kulen ("mountain of the lychees"), north of what would later become Angkor. At the mountainous city of Mahendraparvata, Prince

Jayavarman Ibis took part in a ritual that transformed him from local ruler to "universal monarch." From this point, the king is known only by the name Jayavarman II. But the inscription in the Sdok Kok Thom is more concerned with describing the cult and concept of *devaraja* than with the story of Jayavarman. *Devaraja* is a Sanskrit term that can be translated as "king of the gods," and the ceremony itself was practiced to unite or somehow link the king with Shiva.

Brahmin Hiranyadama, who migrated from India, and Chief Priest Lord Sivakaivalya performed the ritual of *devaraja* to make Jayavarman a *chakravartin*, ruler of the universe. The inscription also tells us that Hiranyadama had magical powers and that he was invited by Jayavarman himself to come and help him release Kambujadesa from Javanese rule. But this *devaraja* ritual wasn't the first time Jayavarman tried to impose himself as the supreme ruler. Other scripts mention that some years earlier, in the southeast, more precisely at the cult site of Ba Phnom, the king took part in another magical ritual. This ritual was probably a part of his conquest preparations.

Jayavarman's origins are somewhere in the southeast of Cambodia, and from there, he conquered his northwestern neighbors. Jayavarman united the conquered territories, which were previously ruled under local kings. According to some historians, Vyadhapura was the first city he took before pushing his way north to Sambhupura. The king imposed himself as the ruler of the territory that is believed to be today's Banteay Prei Nokor, and from there, he launched an attack on Wat Pu, which was a royal city in modern southern Laos. From there, Jayavarman crossed the Dangrek Mountains to arrive in the region where he would start the city of Angkor. He attacked the kings of western Cambodia, but he was unsuccessful in conquering them. In fact, they defeated Jayavarman and forced him to seek refuge at Phnom Kulen. It was during this time that the ritual of *devaraja* took place. Because of this, some historians suggest that Jayavarman performed the ritual so he could consolidate his rule over the conquered regions, as he still faced strong resistance from the west. Nevertheless, the independent kingdom of Kambujadesa was proclaimed during the ceremony, and the conquered rulers accepted Jayavarman as their superior.

According to the scripts, this whole region was previously under the control of the rulers of Java. It is widely believed that these Javanese kings actually came from the island of Java in Indonesia, but there is no evidence to confirm this claim. Alternative suggestions have been made, and some scholars believe that this particular Java could be a place in the Malaysian plains. There are no contemporary inscriptions of Jayavarman's rule, and many scholars believe that he wasn't as important a ruler as later generations made him sound. The Khmer kings that ruled after him left their written admiration of Jayavarman, as they consider him the founder of their empire. Even the Sdok Kok Thom inscription, which is considered the best source for the period of Jayavarman's rule, was carved two centuries after his rule. Some scholars even go so far as to suggest that Angkor wasn't even founded by Jayavarman.

The Sdok Kok Thom inscription also informs us that Jayavarman apparently ruled in five different regions of Cambodia at different periods of his reign. His royal cities changed from Sambor and Hariharalaya to the lost city of Amarendrapura, and that was all before 802 and the proclamation of independence. Amarendrapura is mentioned by name in the scripts, but its location remains a mystery. Some historians suggest already known places as possibilities, such as Banteay Prei Nokor or Kampong Thom, while others believe the city lays as a ruin and has yet to be discovered. It is unknown if Jayavarman built any temples, but several smaller constructions east of Tonle Sap Lake are believed to have been patronized by him.

The inscription from the 10th century suggests that Jayavarman himself came from Java, or at least that he returned from there in 770. But there is no explanation of what he was doing there. Other inscriptions mention him as being of royal descent and that he was twenty years old when he returned to Cambodia. His goal was to end the rule of the Javanese Shailendra dynasty, which possibly ruled only the southern region known as Chenla. Unfortunately, we don't know what compelled Jayavarman to pursue this course of action. It took him thirty years to achieve his goal and be crowned during the *devaraja* ritual at Phnom Kulen. We can only assume that the king used these thirty years to form various alliances through conquests, grants of land, or marriages. He possibly continued to do so after his proclamation as a "universal monarch." This would explain how he got a huge following of powerful and influential people from the region. One of the inscriptions, which are yet to be dated, claims that the borders of Jayavarman's kingdom were China, Champa, the land of cardamoms and mangoes, and the ocean. As you can see, this description of borders is not sufficient to conclude the extension of the kingdom.

Once crowned as the "universal monarch," Jayavarman slowly took over the Angkorian region. The chronology of the inscription suggests it took him around twenty years to conquer this region and assimilate it in Kambujadesa. This period is very poor with evidence, though, as it seems that only several very small and insignificant temples survived. But these years were crucial for the foundation of the Khmer Empire because, at this time, the notion of nationhood and kingship took a different shape, the one that would provide the context for the Khmer Empire through the centuries to come. We can only guess what nationhood meant for the medieval Khmer people. Maybe it was only represented in having a name for their vast kingdom, Kambujadesa, which stood in contrast to the enemy lands. The notion of kingship changed to resemble the relationship of Shiva and other gods. The universal monarch was supreme over all of his people, but he was also there to protect them. These ideas may have been imported from Java, where similar notions of a nation and kingship already existed. But due to the Funan period and the Indian influence on Cambodia, these concepts were already familiar to the local population.

It remains unclear if Jayavarman even intended to unite the Khmer people and create the Cambodians out of them or if this was a mere product of his efforts to overthrow the Shailendra dynasty. Nevertheless, somewhere along the way, the "universal king" managed to create a self-aware community that proved extremely loyal to him. The kings who followed honored Jayavarman as the founder of the nation and the kingdom. They often took a pilgrimage to Hariharalaya (present-day Roluos), where Jayavarman finally settled, to pay him respects as an ancestral founder-spirit, similar to the *Nakta* of the local people. Thus, Jayavarman II became associated with Cambodian territory as its own grand spirit that protects it.

## *Jayavarman's Successors*

There is almost nothing known about Jayavarman's son and successor, Jayavarman III. There is some evidence that he built some of the temples dated to his rule, and one inscription even mentioned that when Jayavarman III failed to hunt an elephant, an unknown deity promised him the beast if he built a temple. Some scholars believe that he also performed the *devaraja* ritual, as the ritual itself became the symbol of legitimate rulers of Cambodia. Jayavarman's III death has been placed to the year 877. This is according to his later successor, Yasovarman I (r. 889–910), who was a very prominent ruler and builder. But even though Yasovarman started an extensive and systematic building program of temples in Hariharalaya, he mentioned his predecessor, Jayavarman III, in only one scripture. In it, he tried to link himself through family ties to none other than Jayavarman II. He claimed to be a relative of a brother to Jayavarman's III grandmother. This grandmother was the mother of Jayavarman's II wife, and it is possible she was connected to the rulers who held the region even before Jayavarman II conquered it. Yasovarman I probably wanted to legitimize his rule by linking himself to the pre-Angkorian rulers of Cambodia, but there is no evidence to explain why he needed this confirmation of his legitimacy.

At first, there was a belief that there were two more kings who ruled between Jayavarman III and Indravarman I, who took the throne directly after Jayavarman III. Their names are Rudravarman and Pṛthivīndravarman. They are mentioned in some Sanskrit scripts from the royal seat at Hariharalaya. However, early translators made a mistake thinking these two names were the names of kings. The inscription has been dated to the rule of Indravarman I's son, Yasovarman I, and is nothing more but a part of his meddling of the royal genealogy. A modern translation discovered that these names were mentioned to explain the family connections between the two royal families. Rudravarman was the younger brother of Jayavarman's III grandmother; however, Pṛthivīndravarman's connection to the royal family remains a mystery, but he might be the same individual as Prithivindreshvara, the father of King Indravarman I. The fact that both of these individuals have the "varman" suffix in their names suggests that they were indeed kings. The title "varman" could be held only by the monarch, but it seems that these two were given the title posthumously with the further purpose to legitimize the rule of the usurper Indravarman I and his son Yasovarman I.

There is evidence that suggests that Yasovarman's immediate predecessor and father, Indravarman I (r. c. 877–889), was the usurper to the Khmer throne, so this might be the reason for his extensive genealogy muddling. Indravarman I was the first Khmer ruler to start the triadic royal behavioral pattern that became a norm for the kings who followed. The first phase was to build an irrigation system in honor of his subjects and the water and soil spirits. Indravarman sponsored the construction of a large water reservoir at Hariharalaya, which was used to trap the rainwater. It covered 300 hectares (approximately 650 acres), and it was known under the name Indratataka. One of the inscriptions found in the vicinity of the reservoir mentions that as soon as Indravarman took the throne, he made a promise he would start digging the irrigation system for the rice fields in only five days.

The temple was attached to the reservoir, with the clear intention to add another layer of meaning to its construction. In the Hindu religion, reservoirs symbolized the ocean or the sacred lakes around the holy mountain. The temple attached to the reservoir was the representation of the holy Mount Meru, where the gods resided. By recreating the geographical features of the sacred mountain and the ocean or lake, the king was able to display his connection with the gods themselves, which only served to raise his prestige. This tradition is also common in northern India. The reservoirs and their temples were also places where the king and his Brahmins would perform various rituals to secure the abundant rice harvest. But the main goal of the reservoirs was a practical one. Throughout the monsoon season, they would collect water that would be released into the rice fields during the dry season. The Indratataka reservoir could hold up to 7.5 million cubic meters of water, and it was the largest reservoir at the time. Later kings built even bigger ones, making Indratataka look very small in comparison.

The second phase of the triadic royal behavioral pattern was the erection of many statues by which the ruler honored his ancestors and his parents. The statues also served as shrines, and the ancestors were given the form of gods. Indravarman built statues for his parents, grandfathers, and great-grandfathers from both his paternal and maternal sides. He also raised statues to Jayavarman II, as he considered him his ancestor, as well as to Jayavarman's wife. All of these statues depicted the embodiment of Shiva and his consorts, and all of Indravarman's statues were built at what is today known as Preah Ko ("the sacred bull") in modern-day Roluos. This city was once the seat of early Khmer kings, and it went by the name Hariharalaya. Preah Ko was built in 879, which makes it the earliest temple built in the royal city. It consists of six towers made out of brick, which was erected in two rows. Both the front and back rows consist of three towers, but the one in the middle front row is the tallest. This tower was dedicated to Jayavarman II, and the two smaller ones next to it were dedicated to Indravarman's father and grandfather. The three towers in the back were dedicated to their respective wives. Indravarman's grandfather was named Rudreshvara, which could be the aforementioned Rudravarman who was posthumously named king by Indravarman's successor.

Preah Ko is important not only because it was the first temple built in Hariharalaya but also because it was the first built in what would become the distinct Khmer architecture of Cambodia. The temple itself was enclosed in a series of moats, and later builders would often imitate this style. The floral engraving and decoration of the temple walls suggest the transfer of the carving style from wood to stone. This is important because it suggests a major social change occurred during the rule of Indravarman, but due to the lack of any other evidence, scholars today could only guess what that change was. The fact that Indravarman's temples were more grandiose than the temples that preceded them speaks about the development of religious ideology, but yet again, the lack of evidence prevents us from understanding it completely. Later kings would overshadow Indravarman's building projects in size and beauty, but it is Preah Ko and Bakong (another temple built by Indravarman) that started the new architectural style.

One of the inscriptions at Preah Ko suggests that Indravarman became a universal monarch by fighting and defeating an unidentified enemy. At that time, Indra, an ancient Hindu deity, was tired of making so many kings, and he made Indravarman a ruler of three worlds. Indravarman's name can be translated to mean "protected by Indra," which would explain the myth behind the scripture. But which three worlds did Indravarman rule? Further examination of the inscriptions found in Rolous has led to the conclusion that he briefly led the armed forces in northeastern Thailand and the Mekong Delta. Another scripture tells a story that Indravarman ruled the lands he conquered and was the greatest king among those of China, Champa, and Java. But this doesn't necessarily mean that Indravarman ruled with higher prestige than the aforementioned kings. It was the poets' duty to decorate the king with skills, metaphors, and virtuous characteristics that would elevate him above his enemies and conceal his flaws.

The third and final phase was the building projects for the temples, which always took the shape of mountains. The king's duty wasn't only to build new temples but also to finish the ones started by his predecessors. Indravarman's temple mountain was Bakong, and it was shaped as a stepped pyramid. Unlike Preah Ko, Bakong was dedicated to Indravarman himself and was to serve his memory after his death. It is believed that these temples erected by the kings were also their burial places. There were at least thirteen kings after Jayavarman II who built these temple mountains, but not all of them survived. At first, these temples were built to resemble the holy Mount Meru, which the myths say lay to the north of the Himalayas and was the center of the universe. Since Mount Meru was the home of the gods, its replicas, in the form of temples, were homes to the king's remains. But the spirits of the kings lived together with the gods on the mythical mountain.

We don't know much about the burial practices of the Khmer Empire this early in its existence. It is presumed the king's body would have been cremated, and the ashes would have been placed in the temple mountains, which served as a sarcophagus. But it might also be that bones were placed there instead of ashes. This is a speculation based on the writings of the Chinese emissary to Angkor from the 13$^{th}$ century, Zhou Daguan. He described a particular practice of the Khmer people, who would throw the bodies of their dead away from the settlement to be eaten by animals. Later, they would come and pick up the bones, but for what purpose remains unknown. Zhou Daguan also attached a certain belief to this ritual. He said that people believed that if the bones were picked clean quickly, the father and mother of the deceased person were blessed. But if the animals didn't consume the body or if they only partially consumed it, this meant that the parents of the deceased were wrongdoers, and this was their punishment. Since ancestral beliefs were very strong, the punishment applied to the ancestor's spirits in case the parents of the deceased were also dead. Zhou Daguan also wrote that the kings were buried in temples, but he didn't mention if they were cremated or not.

Angkorian Khmer didn't practice burying their dead with many possessions, which is very unfortunate for archaeologists. This is also one of the reasons why so little evidence about the Angkorian civilization exists. But one Angkorian graveyard was excavated in the 1960s, located near the Srah Srang reservoir at Angkor. There, numerous cremation jars were excavated with ashes in them. Among the little items buried with the cremation jars were pieces of lead, ceramics, and bronze. This cemetery shows the signs of abandonment and renewal, as the earliest items were dated to the 11th century and the latest to the 15th century. However, there were no similar graveyards found in the vicinity of Bakong and Hariharalaya. It might be that cremation and the burning of ashes became a practice only after the foundation of Angkor.

Bakong was the first Angkorian temple to be built out of stone. The previous temples were usually built out of bricks and perishable materials. There is also a possibility of it being the first temple of pyramidal shape, except for Ak Yom, a temple dating to the 8th century. Unfortunately, Bakong's bas-reliefs were not preserved, and the temple itself was found in very bad shape and needed reconstruction, which was performed by the French in the 1930s.

# Chapter 3 – Yasovarman the Builder and His Successors

Yasovarman I (r. 889-910) was the son of Indravarman and his wife, Indradevi. He was a very important king who left behind many inscriptions and buildings. Some of the inscriptions say that he always dreamt of being greater than his father and that he started the concept of a Cambodian rule centralized around the royal city. Thus, he built his capital, which bore his name until it was abandoned in the 16th century. This capital was Yasodharapura, later known as Angkor. But Yasovarman didn't start building the city as soon as he came to the throne. He started his rule by building more than a hundred monasteries and religious hermitages. Twelve different scriptures mention this building project. Each site was equipped with a royal rest house and a set of regulations that needed to be followed. The buildings were used by the ascetics and by the king himself when he journeyed through his kingdom. The hermitages are known as *ashrams* in Sanskrit, and the term can be translated as a "step on a journey of life." These types of buildings are very common in the Hindu religion and are being built even today.

After building the *ashrams*, Yasovarman constructed an island in his father's reservoir, Indratataka. On this island, he constructed four temples dedicated to his parents. They were built of bricks and were the last temples built in Hariharalaya. Today, they are known as Lolei, which is believed to be a modernized version of the city's name. Scholars believed that the king constructed the island in the middle of the reservoir to symbolize the sacred mountain, which was, according to belief, surrounded by the oceans or lakes. The temple itself had four towers, two in each row. Each row had one tall and one short tower. The tall towers were dedicated to his grandparents, while the short ones were dedicated to his parents. The front row was built to honor the male ancestors, and the back row honors the females.

At the northeast corner of the reservoir, Yasovarman built a raised highway running toward the future site of Angkor, which was around ten miles away (sixteen kilometers). It is possible that there, at the summit of a hill, Yasovarman wanted to build his temple mountain, and because of it, the site was a natural place to build a whole city. He built his temple, Phnom Kandal ("central mountain," today named Phnom Bakheng) as his main temple, and it became one of the central pieces of the Angkor complex. He also built two more temples on the neighboring hills, Phnom Krom and Phnom Bok. The Sdok Kok Thom inscription mentioned that Yasovarman founded the royal city of Shri Yasodharapura, and here, he brought the *devaraja* from Hariharalaya, thus making it a new capital. Only then did he build the "central mountain," Phnom Bakheng.

When the first archaeologists discovered Angkor in the 19th century, Phnom Bakheng wasn't recognized for what it really was: Yasovarman's temple mountain. This discovery was made only in the 1930s when Jean Filliozat, a French scholar, made a detailed study of the temple's symbolism. He discovered that the number of levels, towers, stairways, and statues, when read together or separately, corresponds to various numbers that are considered sacred and metaphysical in Hindu culture. There are seven levels, which symbolically represent the seven heavens of Hinduism. On each level, twelve towers are present, representing the twelve years of Jupiter's journey around the sun. On top of the last level are five towers, positioned so they form a quincunx, one in the middle and four at the edges of the level. This position of the towers symbolized the five mountain peaks of Mount Meru. One hundred eight smaller towers surrounded the whole complex of the temple on the ground level. This number was not picked randomly, as it connects the sun, the moon, and the earth. The average distance of the sun and the moon from the earth is 108 times their respective diameters. The number 108 also represents the lunar cycles, as each has twenty-seven days. But only thirty-three of the towers can be seen from the temple's center, no matter what direction the observer turns to. This number represents the thirty-three gods that resided on the holy Mount Meru. Phnom Bakheng is not just Yasovarman's resting place or a temple. It is an astronomical calendar built in brick and stone. Phnom Bakheng, which was built two centuries before Angkor Wat, was the center of Yasovarman's city of Angkor.

To the east from Phnom Bakheng, a new reservoir was built by the king, and it bore his name. It was called Yasodharatataka, and it was 4 miles long (6.5 kilometers) and 2 miles wide (3 kilometers). The southern shore was reserved for the building of many monasteries, which were dedicated to Shiva, Vishnu, and Buddha. Yasovarman also ordered the construction of various temples across the kingdom, with Prasat Preah Vihear probably being the most notable one after Phnom Bakheng. It was built in the area to the north, where modern Cambodia borders Thailand. The two countries even had a dispute over the ownership of Prasat Preah Vihear, but the International Court of Justice in Hague decided that the temple belongs to Cambodia. But even though the construction of Prasat Preah Vihear started during Yasovarman's reign, the building of the temple itself is attributed to a later king, Suryavarman I. The truth is that many kings built on the site over the ages, and the temple is a mixture of architectural styles, which makes it unique among other Cambodian temples.

The scripts dating from the reign of Yasovarman give us a clue about the magnitude of his empire. The fact that he built temples all over the region he controlled also meant that he commanded a far larger pool of manpower than his predecessors. He was also a cosmopolitan ruler, aware of the grandeur of Indian civilization and tolerant of different religions. Unfortunately, the inscriptions he left behind tell us nothing about his political activity, alliances, or conflicts. There are, however, indications that Yasovarman reformed the law code of the empire so that the fine was levied according to one's ability to pay it. The taxes were efficiently collected, and they were paid in kind and labor throughout the kingdom. The Sanskrit scripts left behind glorify Yasovarman, as it was the tradition, so it is difficult to conclude how successful and efficient a ruler he was. They also fail to inform us of the king's deeds. They serve the purpose only to glorify him with epithets and metaphors. His courage is compared to that of a lion, his rule to the fangs of a beast, and his glory was similar to the roar of the king of the jungle. There is nothing substantial enough that would tell the story of Yasovarman, King of Khmer.

### Jayavarman IV

Yasovarman died in 910, and his two sons succeeded him in turn. There is almost nothing known about the next two kings, Harshavarman I (910–923) and Ishanavarman II (923–928). During their reigns, their uncle, Jayavarman IV, became their political enemy. In 921, he even established his own rule in the city of Koh Ker, some sixty-two miles (one hundred kilometers) north of Angkor. This area was inhospitable, but Jayavarman IV proved his ability to lead, and he started performing kingly duties, such as building a reservoir and a temple mountain. When Ishanavarman II died in 928, Jayavarman IV took the opportunity to proclaim himself the king of the whole Khmer Empire, and he ruled from 928 until 941. His temple mountain is today known as Prasat Thom, and it housed the highest of the lingams in Cambodia except for the one in Angkor Wat. Lingams are symbols of Shiva, more accurately of his phallus inside a yoni (representation of the goddess Shakti's womb). The unification of Shiva and Shakti is a symbolic representation of creation and regeneration. The lingam at Prasat Thom used to be fifty-nine feet high (eighteen meters) and sixteen feet wide (five meters). It was probably made out of metal or at least encased in metal, but sadly, the lingam was not preserved. We only have the scripts describing it.

Koh Ker is a unique city on its own. In old Khmer inscriptions, it is known as Chok Gargyar, and this name is what makes the site unique. It is the only name in the Old Khmer language that we know, mainly because the capitals are always named in Sanskrit. The city was named after the ironwood tree (*Hopea odorata*), which is now called koki. However, the city was also named Lingapura, meaning the "city of lingams." Even when Jayavarman IV became the king, he remained in Koh Ker and made the city his capital. In his scripts, he boasted that his buildings surpassed the grandeur of his predecessors. However, Koh Ker lies largely under jungle overgrowth, so excavations have yet to be done, which will reveal the real magnitude of this city. The monuments Jayavarman IV built are among the largest found throughout Cambodia. Koh Ker alone has around forty temples, of which only eighteen are open to visitors. It is believed that Jayavarman's IV influence extended to northeastern Thailand, as several temples in the Koh Ker style have been found there.

During his reign, the focus of power shifted from the king (raja) to the kingdom (rajya). This shift of political ideology meant that the king had to do what was in the best interest of the kingdom and its people. Because of this, Jayavarman didn't go to war. His reign was the most peaceful period in the Khmer Empire's history, and he used this peace to build his empire. A cultural resurgence occurred, and society, economics, and architecture developed in a unique style. The monumentality of scale in Jayavarman's architecture, as well as the dynamism found in his sculptures, testify of his political identity. He was truly a unique Khmer king, as no one before or after him ruled in complete peace or built such grand buildings.

To build a city filled with forty temples, along with a huge number of monuments, in only twenty years, Jayavarman must have had access to money and a grand labor force. This means that he ruled over a vast empire, as he was able to bring workers from other provinces. The fact that scripts dated to his regnal years were found as far as the Mekong Delta and near Aranyaprathet testify to the extent of his kingdom. The taxes were paid in kind, as the Empire of Angkor never minted coins and didn't use any currency. But besides paying with wax, honey, animals, food, and cloth, the people were able to pay in labor and building materials. This was how Jayavarman managed to gather the workforce to build his city.

### Rajendravarman II (r. 944–968) and Jayavarman V (r. 968–1001)

Jayavarman died in 941, and he was succeeded by one of his sons, Harshavarman II. However, it seems that the succession wasn't peaceful, as the new king ruled for only three years. His uncle, Rajendravarman II, fought him for the throne, managed to usurp it, and ruled the empire until 968. One of the inscriptions dated to his rule tells us how he restored the city of Yasodharapura and adorned its houses with sculptures of gold. Not much is known about Rajendravarman's rule, but he did return the *devaraja* to the old capital, making it a royal city once again. He also reverted to the old customs of building the temples in the middle of lakes, which honored the ancestors. This indicates he wanted to return to the old Angkorian kingship and not continue the ideology Jayavarman IV had started.

Rajendravarman II built many temples, especially in the north of the country. Two of them are especially prominent: the Mebon and Pre Rup, both at Angkor. The two temples are aligned with each other on the north-south axis. While the Mebon is a temple dedicated to the god Shiva, Pre Rup is the king's temple mountain where he was supposedly buried. Its modern name, Pre Rup, means "to turn the body," which comes from an old Cambodian belief that in the burial ceremony, the ashes should be carried around the temple. It is believed that Pre Rup also served as a crematorium for general use.

Although Rajendravarman warred against at least two enemies, his reign was considered to be generally peaceful. The scripts describe the king's abilities in battle and state that his sword was covered in the blood of his enemies, but there are only two mentions of conflict. The first one was against Ramanya. There is no certainty who they were, but scholars believe they could have been a Mons ethnic group of the eastern Dvaravati culture (lasted from 6th century to 11th century). It is believed that the Mons were one of the earliest builders of civilization in Thailand. The second enemy Rajendravarman fought was the Kingdom of Champa in the area between today's Cambodia and Vietnam. One scripture mentions that this last war occurred in 946 when the king took a golden statue from a Cham temple named Po Nagar.

Rajendravarman reigned during the period known for the Khmer Empire's prosperity. This prosperity is reflected in the Sanskrit scriptures left during this time. The Pre Rup stele has almost three hundred stanzas, and each one of them glorifies the king differently, from his genealogy to his wisdom and knowledge to his performances as a king. During his reign, the Khmer Empire commercially expanded to the territories of what is today northeastern Thailand. Trade was established, and with it came cultural influences. Like his predecessors, Rajendravarman was tolerant of Buddhism, and it seems he studied it himself. He even employed Buddhists in his service, for it seems that one of his ministers was one. Unfortunately, his name has been lost to time.

When Rajendravarman II died in 968, he was succeeded by his son, Jayavarman V. But at the time of his father's death, Jayavarman V was just a ten-year-old boy, and the state politics were run by his close family and high officials. We know of this because the family members left many scriptures behind them. At this point, the building of temples and statues wasn't only the duty of a king but of everyone involved in running the state. One of the most beautiful temples at Angkor, known as the Banteay Srei ("fortress of women"), was built during the reign of Jayavarman V, but the main builder was the king's relative and guru, Yajnavaraha. In fact, he was the grandson of King Harshavarman I and served as the royal doctor to Rajendravarman II. When the boy-king came to the throne, Yajnavaraha became his tutor and mentor. Yajnavaraha was a Vedic scholar, and many scripts praise his kindness and help to the poor. For his efforts to relieve the poverty across the kingdom, the guru received a present from the king, a parasol made out of peacock's feathers.

But Yajnavaraha wasn't the only one listed as the builder of Banteay Srei. His younger brother, Vishnukumura, was also listed as one of the people who commissioned the construction. Although they came from a royal family and were part of the aristocracy, they were not able to afford such extensive building projects. Because of this, the king's sister, Jahavi, was involved in the project, and she helped her cousins raise the money for the construction of the temple. Banteay Srei is a major temple in Angkor and was dedicated to Shiva. Its original name was *Tribhuvanamahesvara* ("the great lord of the threefold world"). But the temple is a complex of buildings, and while some are devoted to Shiva, others are devoted to Vishnu. The modern name of the temple, Banteay Srei, was given to the temple because of its beautiful and delicate bas-reliefs that resemble elaborate lace patterns. During the 11$^{th}$ century, the temple was rebuilt and expanded by later kings, and it remained in use at least until the late 14$^{th}$ century.

The king's sister wasn't the only female member of the royal family involved in public work. Women of the Khmer Empire were emancipated enough to take high offices, and their wisdom was often praised by foreign ambassadors. This might have been due to the influence of Buddhist teachings, which were spreading throughout the kingdom at the time. Buddha considered all people equal, and it was probably these teachings that ushered women to take on the challenge of statesmanship. Prana, another royal family member, was known for her position as the king's advisor. The Chinese scripts mention how Cambodian women of the period were emancipated and even took the positions of judges.

Jayavarman ruled in peace for the next thirty years, and no major events mark his reign. But when he died in 1001, the next few years were very destructive. The throne was succeeded by Udayadityavarman I, the maternal nephew of Jayavarman V. However, the new king reigned for only a few months before he died. Whether his death was natural or violent, we will never know. But we do know it started a civil war in the Khmer Empire, which lasted for the next nine years. His successor was Jayaviravarman, and his origins remain a mystery. Some scholars believe he was the brother of Udayadityavarman; therefore, he would have been a rightful heir to the throne. Others believe he was a usurper, maybe even a prince from Thailand's city of Tambralinga. He ruled from 1002 until 1011, and after the civil war, he simply disappears from the inscriptions.

## Suryavarman I (r. 1006–1050)

After the death of King Jayavarman V, Suryavarman defeated the armies of Udayadityavarman I and proclaimed himself the king. However, Jayaviravarman claimed the throne too, and even though he took Angkor, the rest of the kingdom wasn't under his control. Suryavarman I was firmly established in the north. From there, he would launch sporadic warfare with his southern counterpart. He also formed various alliances, coalitions, and marriages throughout the kingdom, securing the support of the majority of the people. The process of his establishment as the king of the whole Khmer territory resembled that of Jayavarman II, two centuries before. It is possible that Suryavarman even had powerful allies within the priestly family of Angkor, which enabled him to eventually defeat Jayaviravarman and take his throne. Some scholars suggest that all of the previous kings that came after Jayavarman V were usurpers and that they weren't even Cambodians. According to them, Suryavarman was a local Cambodian ruler who wanted to get rid of the usurpers, although he wasn't a member of the previous royal dynasty that ruled from Angkor.

By 910, Suryavarman had defeated his enemies and established himself as king in Angkor. With his rule came a religious shift. The new king wasn't a Buddhist, but he is known for his patronage of Buddhism. Even his posthumous name, *Nirvanapada* ("the king who reached nirvana"), is an acknowledgment of his respect for this religion. Some hostile inscriptions accuse Suryavarman of destroying the religious iconography. However, if Suryavarman was of some other religion than Hinduism, the destruction of iconography would have been far more extensive. Another inscription claims that Suryavarman took away the properties and fortunes of the elite family members, as they had become rich and powerful enough to pose a threat to his rule. It seems that Suryavarman was on the constant lookout for threats, which could mean he was, indeed, a usurper.

Upon his arrival to Yasodharapura, Suryavarman demanded that all the religious and state officials swear a loyalty oath to him. More than four thousand officials gathered at the newly constructed palace to obey him. The oath they took survived in a lengthy inscription, and it ends with a threat of permanent hell for all those who break the oath. However, those who proved loyal would be rewarded with high offices, and food would be provided for their families.

Suryavarman led expansionist politics. He conquered and annexed the territories to the west. The Tonle Sap was colonized with new religious foundations, and the Theravada Buddhist kingdom of Louvo was absorbed by the Empire of Angkor. All of this led to an increase in the population, especially in the cities. The king had to expand the irrigation network to meet the demands for water. But often, Suryavarman had to defend his kingdom. There is evidence that suggests the Khmer king was forced to ask Chola Emperor Rajaraja I of Tamil Nadu (southern India) for help against the Tambralinga kingdom of the Malay Peninsula. The Tambralinga kingdom was aided by King Sangrama Vijayatungavarman of the Srivijaya kingdom (based on Sumatra). The Khmer Empire won, but this conflict led to another major one between the Chola dynasty and the Srivijaya kingdom in 1025.

Under Suryavarman's rule, the priestly and bureaucratic offices were institutionalized. But even then, they were seldom separated in practice. Government-sponsored religious foundations were used to collect revenue, but it remains obscure in what ways. However, scholars suspect that the major role was played by the powerful priestly-bureaucratic families that were close to the king. The administration of Suryavarman's kingdom focused on urbanization. The inscriptions of Suryavarman's three immediate predecessors mention the existence of twenty urban centers, which all used the suffix *pura*, which is Sanskrit for "city." This word is still in use throughout Southeast Asia and can be seen in the names of cities such as Jaipur in India or Singapore ("Lion City"). During the reign of Suryavarman, the number of cities increased to forty-seven. This means that Suryavarman led a policy of herding his subjects into tight communities. He probably uprooted them from rural areas that were hard to reach and administrate. There is a possibility that many of these settlements were cities only by name, with the intention behind it being to raise the prestige of local elite families. However, Suryavarman is responsible for the heavy urbanization of the kingdom, as other evidence suggests it too.

Some of the inscriptions that refer to King Suryavarman describe the development of local and overseas trade. Throughout Cambodian history, merchants were usually outsiders. They were native to China, Vietnam, or India, and this didn't change during the reign of Suryavarman. However, the references toward these merchants suddenly jumped in frequency. Foreign trade was largely based on exchanging wild forest goods, such as fruit and timber, for items produced by various civilizations, such as ceramics, cloth, and porcelain. However, there is evidence of trade with land, rice, domestic animals, and slaves, which were all imported from other countries. Interestingly enough, medieval Cambodians refused to implement any kind of currency, and all trade was paid in kind.

Suryavarman's urbanization of the kingdom and his ability to move and administrate the people marks a departure from the past when the economy relied on rural life. Agriculture changed too, as suddenly, one harvest per year wasn't enough to produce food for the whole kingdom. Previously, the majority of the people were commoners, and they needed less food to survive. But now, the state became a machine run by the apparatus of priests, royal family members, high officials, bureaucrats, and the army, and they all needed to be fed. The people now had to produce food all year round, a system that would remain implemented in the Khmer Empire through the reigns of the kings to come.

Suryavarman I is also remembered for the expansion work he performed on some of the already existing temples, such as Banteay Srei, Phnom Chisor, Prasat Preah Vihear, and Wat Ek Phnom. Wat Ek Phnom was used as a royal residence by the later kings. But he also built new constructions, and among the most famous was the West Baray reservoir, which was able to hold 123 million liters of water. Perhaps it was not finished during Suryavarman's reign, but West Baray remains the largest reservoir of the Khmer Empire that survived history. Suryavarman also started construction on Preah Khan Kompong Svay, around sixty-two miles (one hundred kilometers) east of Angkor. With its exterior enclosure taking up the territory of five square kilometers, it is the largest temple complex that was dated to the Angkorian era.

When Suryavarman died in 1050, he was succeeded by Udayadityavarman II (r. 1050–1066). But this new king was not Suryavarman's son. He was probably a descendant of Yasovarman I. Udayadityavarman II is remembered for finishing the construction of West Baray. However, unlike Suryavarman I, the new Khmer king didn't reign in peace. There were several rebellions, of which two were dated to 1051 and 1065. The first rebellion is described on inscriptions found at the Baphuon temple, and it mentions that the leader was a certain Aravindahrada, who was probably a vassal king of Cambodia. The king sent several military expeditions against Aravindahrada, but they all failed. Finally, when Udayadityavarman sent his loyal general named Sangrama, the rebel was defeated. The inscriptions mention Aravindahrada ran to Champa after the defeat. The second rebellion in 1065 was led by Kamvau, who was also one of the king's favorite generals. The battle between Kamvau and Sangrama is described in one of the inscriptions, and it seemed that Kamvau managed to wound Sangrama with an arrow. But Sangrama shot three arrows at his enemy, piercing his head, neck, and heart. There was also a third rebellion, led by a local chief named Slvat. However, the date of this battle is not known with certainty. It most likely occurred in 1066, as this was the last year of Utyadityavarman's reign. Slvat had the help of his younger brother, Siddhikara, and a hero named Sagantibhuvana. Again, Sangrama managed to defeat the rebels, bind them in chains, and present them to the king.

# Chapter 4 – Suryavarman II and Angkor Wat

Bas-relief depicting King Suryavarman I

The last years of the 11$^{th}$ century in Cambodia were marked by constant turmoil and a fight for power. At some moments, three kings claimed to be the absolute ruler at the same time. Nevertheless, a new dynasty rose to power in Angkor, and it would last for more than a hundred years. Little is known about the first two kings of this new dynasty: Jayavarman VI (r. 1080-1107) and his elder brother Dharanindravarman I (1107-1113). Jayavarman VI fought Udayadityavarman II's successor, Harshavarman III (r. 1066-1080), and he managed to defeat him only because the kingdom was attacked on many sides. During the reign of Harshavarman III, the Khmers had to fight off an invasion from neighboring Champa, as well as from the Chinese Song dynasty. Finally, when faced with Jayavarman VI, who came from the Phimai area in present-day Thailand, the kingdom was already exhausted. Jayavarman VI managed to usurp the throne.

It is possible Jayavarman VI used to be a vassal prince of Cambodia, and he saw the opportunity to take the throne after the kingdom was exhausted by the constant turmoil and wars. He founded a new dynasty in Angkor, the Mahidharapura, named after his ancestral home in the Mun River Valley. The inscription found in the Phanom Rung, the temple on the edge of a volcano in Thailand, speaks about the ancient kingdom of Mahidharapura, which was probably annexed by Angkor at one point. Jayavarman VI claimed ancestry from the mythical hermit Kambu Swayambhuva, who married a nymph named Mera. His descendants were the Kambuja (Kamboja) tribe, which gave the kingdom of Kambujadesa and, therefore modern, Cambodia its name.

For the first several years of his reign, Jayavarman VI had to fight the followers of the previous king, Harshavarman III, who remained loyal to the old Angkor royal line. It is even possible that Nripatindravarman, a successor of Harshavarman III, reigned in Angkor until 1113 and that Jayavarman never really managed to usurp the Angkorian throne itself. This claim is supported by an inscription that claims Suryavarman II (r. 1113–1150) took the kingship of two kings. One was his uncle, Dharanindravarman I, who succeeded Jayavarman VI. The other one remains unnamed, but it could very well be Nripatindravarman.

Following the death of Jayavarman VI, Dharanindravarman I succeeded the throne. He married his younger brother's wife, Queen Vijayendralakshmi. There is nothing else known about the reign of this king except that he died in battle, which was fought against his great-nephew, Suryavarman II.

### Suryavarman II (r. 1113–1150)

Suryavarman II was the first unifying king since Udayadityavarman II. After defeating his great-uncle, Dharanindravarman I, on the battlefield, he rose as a ruler of the unified principalities of Cambodia. He shared a name with Suryavarman I, although they were not related at all. However, the parallel between the two kings doesn't end with their names. Just like his predecessor, Suryavarman II came to power after a period of disorder, fragmentation, and internal rebellions. Once he took Yasodharapura, Suryavarman I and II both responded to disorder with vigorous administrative policies, pragmatic kingship, and expansion of territory. Suryavarman II led his forces to the east against the Champa. But these expeditions were largely unsuccessful, and the territory he gained wasn't much at all. However, it did bring new people under his control, people who would be used as a workforce behind his great building projects.

Suryavarman was crowned twice, both times by the same priest, who was named Divakarapandita. The first coronation took place in 1113, but scholars can't agree on whether Suryavarman had conquered both claimants to the throne or just Nripatindravarman. Suryavarman's second coronation ceremony took place in 1119, and some historians believe this ceremony took place because Suryavarman finally defeated Dharanindravarman I. However, the inscriptions are not clear on this matter, and it is possible that the second coronation was nothing more but the affirmation of his authority after the seizure of some Champa territory.

Suryavarman was the first king to establish diplomatic relations with China. The first embassy was sent to the Song court in 1116, where the details of trade between the two nations were discussed. The embassy stayed in China for only one year, but two more were sent in 1120 and 1128. One of the Chinese texts mentions that the Cambodian king was a great Chinese vassal. However, it is unclear if Suryavarman ever thought of himself as a servant to the Song dynasty. After all, it is no secret the Chinese emperors thought the whole world was under their vassalage.

Suryavarman warred against Vietnam and Champa because he was persuaded to do so by the Chinese. The king also used mercenaries from the western Cambodian territories in these fights and possibly even the Champa people in his attacks on Vietnam's Nghe An Province. The evidence suggests that Suryavarman was unsuccessful in his military attempts. In 1128, he sent around twenty thousand soldiers in an attack on Dai Viet, a Vietnamese kingdom. Suryavarman was easily defeated and had to flee for his life. In 1132, Suryavarman again attempted to take Dai Viet, this time by the sea. He sent seven hundred vessels, which were filled with both Khmer and Champa men, but once again, he was unsuccessful. Another expedition was sent in 1145, but King Jaya Indravarman III of Champa refused to help him, as he already made peace with the Vietnamese ruling Ly dynasty. Nevertheless, Suryavarman made one last attempt in 1150. He was defeated and had to withdraw his conquered army back to Cambodia.

Because Suryavarman II didn't want to be associated with his immediate predecessors, as they had led the kingdom into disorder, he sought to separate himself from them in religious terms. Suryavarman I did something similar when he chose to support Buddhism, but Suryavarman II did something even more drastic. He turned to Vishnu, making him the supreme deity instead of the previously worshiped Shiva. The king built some of the most impressive temples in northeastern Thailand, such as Phimai and Phanom Rung. His devotion to Vishnu inspired him to build the largest and most beautiful of all Cambodian temples: Angkor Wat. But Angkor Wat was more than just a temple. It was a monument, a tomb, and an observatory. Today, it is one of the most visited places in the world.

Suryavarman II was the first Cambodian king who was depicted in an image. His image in Angkor Wat shows him sitting on an elaborate throne that had nagas ("snakes") instead of legs. The king himself is adorned with jewelry, such as earrings, bracelets, anklets, and armlets. In one hand, he holds a dead snake, but the symbolism behind this remains a mystery. The king's depiction is a part of a large scene that portrays court life. The scene is set amid a forest filled with attendants, princesses, Brahmins, advisors, and slaves. Suryavarman II was married, and his wife is mentioned in some of the inscriptions, but her name has been lost.

Suryavarman died in 1150 during the military campaign against Champa. He was succeeded by his cousin, Dharanindravarman II (r. 1150–1160), who was a weak ruler and who allowed the kingdom to enter yet another phase of internal feuding. Dharanindravarman married Princess Sri Jayarajacudamani. She was the daughter of King Harshavarman III. Their son, Jayavarman VII, is remembered for his devotion to Buddhism.

### Angkor Wat

Angkor Wat is the temple that stands on Cambodia's national flag and is the symbol of the state, culture, and religion. It stands on 162.6 hectares of land, which makes it the world's biggest religious monument. Its construction began in the early 12th century during the reign of King Suryavarman II, who wanted a temple and a tomb for himself and his main deity, the Hindu god Vishnu. However, Angkor Wat was not completed during Suryavarman's life. The central piece of the temple, the now-lost statue of Vishnu, was erected in July 1131.

Scholars believe this occurred on the king's thirty-third birthday, a number with great cosmic meaning in Hinduism as there are thirty-three Vedic deities.

Angkor Wat is unlike any other Cambodian temple, and it bears a veil of mystery. First of all, it is open to the west, while the rest of the temples are oriented toward the east. This might be because Angkor Wat was originally dedicated to Vishnu, who is often associated with the west. Cambodia's previous main deity, Shiva, is associated with the east, and all of the other temples are therefore east-oriented. And if one is to follow the bas-relief that spreads more than a mile around the outer walls of the temple, he would have to start moving counterclockwise, starting from the northwestern corner of the temple. All the other temples follow a clockwise orientation when it comes to reading the bas-reliefs, which would keep the relief on the person's right side at all times. This custom is even known in Sanskrit under the name *pradakshina* ("to the right"). But the western orientation and the counterclockwise direction is nothing new in Hinduism or the Cambodian culture. However, these practices are always associated with the dead. It is possible that because of this custom, the modern word for the west also means "to sink" or "to drown." Because of all this, some scholars believe that the primal function of Angkor Wat was to be a tomb. George Coedès, a French scholar, was the first one to suggest that Angkor Wat's orientation to the west might be connected to Vishnu, not death. But he didn't deny it could also be a tomb, as it does contain several receptacles that perhaps functioned as sarcophagi.

The original name of Angkor Wat is unknown as the foundation stele was never found. It is also odd that none of the contemporary inscriptions of Cambodia refer to this temple. Its modern name, Angkor Wat, means "temple city" or the "city of temples." Some scholars believe the old name may have been *Varah Vishnu-lok* or VARAHA VISHNU-LOK, as the temple was dedicated to Vishnu and King Suryavarman II. The king's posthumous name was

*Paramavishnuloka,* which means "the king who has gone to the supreme world of Vishnu." Since the temple also served as his tomb, the suggested name *Varah Vishnu-lok* is probable. *Varah,* or *Varaha,* is the wild boar avatar of Vishnu, while *Vishnu-lok* means "world of Vishnu."

Angkor Wat wasn't investigated in detail by scholars until the 1980s. This was due to World War II, the Cambodian Civil War, and the Khmer Rouge; the latter cut off the temple from the rest of the world. But the people who were allowed access brought back images and written descriptions, allowing scientists and scholars insight into the mysteries that were being kept secret in Cambodia. Eleanor Mannikka started her study of the temple's dimensions in the mid-1970s based on existing photographs of Angkor Wat. She was convinced that the learned Khmer designers of the temple had encoded it. She was the first to determine that the Cambodian measurement used at Angkor, *hat,* was equivalent to 1.3 feet (0.4 meters). She then asked herself how many *hat* were in the important dimensions of the temple, such as the distance between the western entrance and the central tower. Since the western entrance was the only one that had a causeway, its importance as a landmark was obvious. Eleanor Mannikka concluded that this distance was 1,728 *hat.* Other measurements of the important landmarks on the same axis came up with the results of 1,296 *hat,* 867 *hat,* and 439 *hat.* Eleanor Mannikka concluded that these numbers correspond to the four ages of the world, or *yuga* in Sanskrit. The first in the *yuga* cycle is *Satya Yuga* (the golden age), in which the people are ruled by the gods. It lasts for 1,728,000 years. The second one is *Treta Yuga,* a period in which Vishnu's three avatars would be seen. It lasts for 1,296,000 years. The third *yuga* is *Dvapara Yuga,* or the age of compassion and truthfulness. It lasts for 864,000 years. The fourth and last period is *Kali Yuga,* in which strife and quarrel rule. This is why this period bears the name of the demon Kali. It lasts for 432,000 years. According to Hinduism, we are living in *Kali Yuga* at the moment. Once it ends, the world as we know it will be destroyed and rebuilt into a new golden age, and the cycle will repeat.

Eleanor Mannikka claims that the fact that the four ages closely correlate with the particular distances along the east-west axis of the temple is proof enough that Angkor Wat is coded and can be read in terms of time and space. The distance one must traverse from the main entrance to the central statue of Vishnu coincides with the *yuga* cycle and the stages one must metaphorically go through in life. Since west is seen as the direction in which the dead walk, going the opposite direction, along the west-east axis, means moving back in time. Thus, one would be approaching the golden age, at least according to Hinduism.

Mannikka worked closely with astronomers, and together, they came to interesting conclusions about the astronomical correlations of the frequently recurring distances of the Angkor Wat landmarks. The most interesting one is that if an observer stands at the western entrance on the morning of the summer solstice, he will see that the sun rises precisely above the central tower of the temple. This is important for Suryavarman II, whose name means "protected by the sun." Another interesting conclusion modern astronomers have come to is that on any other day, the sunrise aligned with the axis between the western gate and a small hill to the northeast named Phnom Bok.

Modern scholars compare the magnificence and architecture of Angkor Wat to the temples of ancient Greece or Rome. The main building material in the 12th century was sandstone, and the whole temple was built with sandstone blocks. The binding for the blocks still intrigues scholars as it's unknown what they used. Some think slaked lime was used, while others propose natural resins. The temple itself is typical for Khmer architecture, and it consists of lotus bud-shaped towers, the ogival half galleries, and broad passageways. The main decorative elements of the temple are bas-reliefs that depict narrative scenes, garlands, and devatas (spirits or lesser deities). Unfortunately, many of these elements were destroyed during the civil wars in Cambodia or by looters. The thieves even took some of the reconstructed figures in the hopes they could sell them as originals.

The statue of Vishnu, which is believed to have once occupied the center of the temple, was found under the southern tower. It was probably moved outside by Buddhists, who still occupy the temple. Angkor Wat is surrounded by an outer wall that is over 14.5 feet (4.5 meters) high and encloses over 203 acres (820,000 square meters), as well as a moat that is around 623 feet (190 meters) wide. The access to the temple is made out of an earthen bank and a gateway, but there are other side entrances that are big enough for elephants to pass through. Because of this, they are called "elephant gates." The temple was part of a city that also had a royal palace. However, since only the temples were built from stone, none of the other buildings were preserved. The outlines of some streets can still be seen, but nothing else except the temple itself remains.

Angkor Wat stands on a platform, raised above what was once a city. It has three galleries rising to the central tower. Each level is higher than the previous one, and they were maybe even dedicated to the king, the moon, and Vishnu. However, the temple is best known for its bas-reliefs. The inner wall of the outer gallery depicts the scenes from the *Ramayana* and *Mahabharata*. The western gallery displays the scenes of the Battle of Lanka (from the *Ramayana*) and the Battle of Kurukshetra (from the *Mahabharata*). The southern gallery wall displays a historical scene, the procession of Suryavarman II, followed by the thirty-two hells and thirty-seven heavens of Hindu religion. The eastern gallery displays one of the most famous scenes, the Samudra Manthan (the churning of the sea of milk). In this scene, Vishnu instructs ninety-two asuras (demigods) and eighty-eight devas (divinities) to churn the sea by using the body of Vasuki, a serpent king.

Angkor Wat underwent restoration works in 1986 and 1992. It is still undergoing various reconstruction projects, but it is mainly a tourist attraction. The Cambodian government protects the site, and it became a part of the UNESCO World Heritage List in 1992. In 2018, the temple saw 7,300 tourists every day of the year, making it a total of 2.6 million people. Luckily, there are no examples of tourists damaging the site, except for a few cases of graffiti. To protect the temple itself, the Cambodian government invested in ropes and wooden steps, and approximately 28 percent of the ticket revenue is reserved for temple maintenance. At least five tourists per year are caught taking nude photographs on the site of Angkor Wat, and for that, they were immediately deported from Cambodia, as they broke the moral values of this Buddhist state.

# Chapter 5 – Jayavarman VII

Bust of King Jayavarman VII as Buddha

The evidence suggests that Suryavarman II led a campaign in Vietnam as late as 1150, but it is unknown when he exactly died. There are no inscriptions preserved from the period between 1145 and 1182, so the history of this period must be reconstructed from what the later kings left behind. It is believed that one of Suryavarman's cousins staged a coup d'état and took the throne. His name was Dharanindravarman II (r. c. 1150–1160), and it appears he was a Buddhist. But it is unclear if he ever ruled from Yasodharapura. According to one inscription dated to Jayavarman VII, Dharanindravarman was succeeded by Yasovarman II. This inscription tells how Yasovarman II put an end to the rebellion somewhere in the north, but it remains a mystery who the people who rebelled were. In the bas-relief of Banteay Chhmar, they were depicted as people with animal heads. This led scholars to believe that the revolt was directed by those who belonged to the bottom of society. This was probably why they were depicted in such a way, as they were the lowest of the low. To the elites, these people would have been on the same level as animals.

Instability in the Khmer Empire continued throughout the 1160s, for it seems Yasovarman II was assassinated by one of his subordinates, Tribhuvanadityavarman, who proceeded to declare himself a king. There is also the absence of inscriptions from this period, which can only be explained by rapid changes and the questionable legitimacy of the rulers. This instability may be a result of the faltering of the hydraulic organization of the kingdom. The system of reservoirs and canals, which were the basis of Angkor's rice economy, started diminishing during the reign of Suryavarman II. Even Angkor Wat was built with much smaller hydraulic components than those of earlier temples. Hydraulic-based cities were still built in the mid-12th century but at a considerable distance from Angkor, at Beng Mealea and Kompong Svay. It is believed that the water sources of the Angkor region were exhausted due to population growth. Even the network of streams and canals that brought water from Phnom

Kulen was diverted to supply the ever-growing population. This means that by the time water reached the fields, it was deprived of all the nutrients needed to grow rice. During the dry periods, these canals were probably dried out or became bodies of stagnant water. This stagnation might have even brought malaria upon the citizens of the Angkor region, further destabilizing the kingdom. However, since there is no written evidence, these theories are just speculations.

### Jayavarman VII (r. 1811–1218)

Jayavarman VII was the son of Dharanindravarman II and Queen Sri Jayarajacudamani. However, it seems that Jayavarman wasn't a completely legitimate successor to the throne, as he felt compelled to make inscriptions explaining his early life or at least what he wanted the people to believe of his life. Nevertheless, some scholars believed that he was the pinnacle of Khmer kingship despite his less legitimate claim to the throne. The inscriptions Jayavarman VII left behind tell us about his radical changes and his departure from tradition. It is because of this radicalism that Jayavarman VII dominates the historiography of Cambodia.

Like his father, Jayavarman was a Buddhist. He may have been a cousin of Suryavarman II, as he also belonged to the so-called Mahidharapura dynasty. However, some scholars doubt Jayavarman was the son of Dharanindravarman because this fact is very poorly documented. Nevertheless, Jayavarman did serve a role in the court of Yasovarman, but between 1166 and 1177, he lived away from the Angkor region. A statue of him in the Preah Kham temple in Kompong Svay, where the city of Jayadityapura is located, was found, and it is dated to the period before his reign. Maybe that is where he spent those years away from Angkor. But there is also evidence that he spent some time in Champa. This makes some scholars think that Jayadityapura was a rival city of Angkor or maybe its vassal. The questions of how Jayavarman was related to the usurper king Tribhuvanadityavarman, who came after Yasovarman, and what he was doing in Champa remain unanswered.

Jayavarman was a Buddhist king, and he followed the teachings of Mahayana Buddhism. He did his best to integrate Buddhist beliefs with the Cambodian kingship doctrines. Therefore, he practiced Buddhist kingship, which was different in several ways from the Hindu kingship Khmer was used to. In Hinduism, it is believed that a king, dead or alive, enjoyed a particular relationship with one of the Hindu deities, whether that was Shiva, Vishnu, or the composite of the two known as Harihara. The king would always dedicate his temple mountain to the deity he revered, and the kings used this special relationship with the gods to explain their power and grandeur. But the people believed that their power was what secured their relationship with the divine and thus secured regular rainfall. This was why Cambodians believed a king was necessary. Due to his ability to talk to the gods, the king had to be isolated. He distanced himself from the people and locked himself in his grand palace. He was both the master and victim of this kingship system. He enjoyed the power and wealth, and he was the central figure to whom the people pled for favors, titles, and rights. But he was alone, and he rarely had the welfare of his people in mind when making decisions, as he had to work for the benefit of the kingdom as a whole, which most of the time meant exploiting his subjects.

The Buddhist kingdom grew out of the Hindu model (after all, Buddha was an Indian prince), but some of the elements of the rule were modified under Jayavarman VII. The king was no longer seen as having a special relationship with one of the gods, and he would not join the divines after his death. Instead, Jayavarman believed that he needed to redeem himself through devotion to Buddhist teachings and through the performance of good deeds. Still, Jayavarman never sought to deconstruct the Cambodian belief system or get rid of the existing social structures. He didn't ban Hindu institutions, such as Brahmanism, slavery, or even kingship. He was extremely tolerant of Hinduism, and he used it to build his vision of kingship. After all, he was a 12<sup>th</sup>-century king, and slavery and social discord were a norm at that time.

The main difference between the Hindu and Buddhist kingships was how the ruler viewed his subjects. In Hindu tradition, the king performed various rituals, built temples, arranged marriages, and produced inscriptions and poems that celebrated his grandeur and godliness. But he did all of this without an audience. People were devoid of the knowledge of what lay behind the rituals and what was in the poems and inscriptions. To the king, the number of his subjects was what mattered most. The more people he ruled, the greater a king he was. Buddhist kings, on the other hand, used their subjects as an audience, objects of their compassion, and as the element of their redemption. It was through his subjects and by performing good deeds that a Buddhist king could redeem his soul from the misdeeds of his past lives.

Jayavarman was married to Princess Jayarajadevi, and after her death, he married her sister, Indradevi. It is believed that these two women were the main influences on not only his devotion to Buddhism but also his reign. However, some scholars believe that an event that preceded Jayavarman's coronation determined the course of his reign. This was the invasion of Champa in 1177, and Jayavarman's whole reign was a response to this attack. It was mentioned earlier that Jayavarman spent some time during the 1160s in Champa. This fact has led historians to believe that the young Jayavarman was out of favor with the Cambodian court, where he had previously served. Maybe he was even exiled. This suggestion is backed by the fact that he dared to come back to Angkor only after the death of Yasovarman II. Even in later inscriptions, Jayavarman rarely speaks of the events of his formative years, which might mean that he had nothing to boast about.

The reasons why Champa attacked Cambodia are elusive because the inscriptions tend to make the connection between any aggressiveness with neighbors to royal ambitions, treachery, and revenge. In 1177, King Jaya Indravarman IV of Champa attacked Cambodia by land, and a year later, he invaded by water, sailing his fleet up the Mekong River. They crossed the Tonle Sap Lake and used the tributary Siem Reap River to approach Yasodharapura. King Tribhuvanadityavarman was killed, and the city was pillaged. One of the inscriptions mentions that King Jaya Indravarman didn't want to listen to any peace proposals. Jayavarman VII took the opportunity to lead the Khmer defensive army, and they managed to expel the invaders from the kingdom. The bas-relief of the Bayon and Banteay Chhmar depict the naval battle between Jayavarman and the Champa army. Although Jayavarman claimed he killed Jaya Indravarman, some of the inscriptions suggest it was another Khmer prince.

Finally, when Jayavarman arrived in Angkor after the invasion, he found the region in disorder. The factions were fighting between themselves and supporting different candidates for the throne. The people also took the opportunity of anarchy to steal and plunder. One of Jayavarman's wives left an inscription in which she claims how before her husband's rule, the land was divided between many rulers and suffered greatly from this fracture. She further describes how Jayavarman united the people under his own rule and brought security and stability to the kingdom. Jayavarman was crowned king between 1181 and 1183 (the exact date is unknown). The kingdom he inherited was ruined thanks to his immediate predecessors, but through his faith, victories in battles, and his ability to judge justly, Jayavarman liberated Angkor from its past. However, the period between the victory over Champa and his coronation is empty, devoid of any inscriptions. It must have been a period of political negotiations and maybe even further conflicts with local chieftains. Once Jayavarman was on the throne, he wanted to reform the kingdom, and he saw himself as the main instrument of this transformation.

The building program of Jayavarman VII was a hasty one. He built a lot and fast. He built everything, from roads to temples to reservoirs. Many of the projects he started had to be finished after his death, but because he built so much and so fast, most of the buildings were done sloppily. He also used up the local supplies of limestone and sandstone, which had been used in building Angkor Wat. His inscriptions say that thousands of people worked on his building projects. Furthermore, it concludes that Jayavarman thought that labor would remove his people from the suffering in which they were entrenched. Although he didn't specify what exactly that suffering was, he did mention that he could feel the physical pain of his subjects. He felt this as spiritual pain; therefore, it was on a higher level, meaning he felt more than his own subjects did. This is in accordance with the Buddhist teachings, which places suffering as related to a purpose in life. Physical suffering is less important because it's just that—physical.

Jayavarman appears to be a compassionate king due to this belief, but did Jayavarman have only the best interests of his people in mind at all times? There is a certain duality in his persona and in the depictions of him as a king. All the bas-relief scenes that depict his battle against the Chams show him as a ruthless, bloodthirsty, and almost tyrannical leader. But his statues and the inscriptions that mention him depict him as a calm, serene, and wise man who lived an ascetic life. The extensive roadbuilding that he performed may have been connected with the military expeditions he engaged, but it also may have been that the roads were needed for easier transport of goods to port towns and China. However, Jayavarman was also in his late fifties when he took the throne, and it might be that he built extensively and with haste because he was racing against time. He wanted to leave behind at least as much as his predecessors, if not even more, but he had considerably less time to do so.

Not much is known about the early years of Jayavarman's reign, except that he considerably expanded the kingdom. It is believed that this expansion helped him gain the support of elite classes, as the Brahmins were aware of the benefits the expansion brought to the kingdom. By the beginning of the 13th century, Laos, Thailand, and Champa were paying tribute to Angkor, which was an enormous accomplishment for a new king, especially one who had started from the low position of a simple court official and one who had probably been disfavored too. However, his accomplishments brought him the support of at least part of the people. There was an uprising in the north that had to be dealt with, but other than that, Jayavarman ruled his kingdom without much internal trouble. However, he was a Buddhist king, and his Hindu elite class must have felt some kind of resentment toward him. This is especially seen in the anti-Buddhist iconoclasm that occurred in Cambodia after Jayavarman's death.

Jayavarman was also an innovative king. He was the first one to build hospitals, constructing around 102 of them. According to the stele of Ta Prohm, the first four were built at the gates of Angkor Thom, as well as to the west of Angkor in the area of modern-day northeastern Thailand. Some were even built as far as today's Laos. The hospitals served 838 villages, and steles were carved upon the foundation of the hospitals, which give details about their administration. Unlike his predecessors, Jayavarman gave special notice to public works. While earlier kings mentioned only the building of reservoirs as public works, Jayavarman thought that the construction of roads, hospitals, and bridges was equally important. Another important public construction work of Jayavarman's reign was the "houses of fire." The exact purpose of these buildings is unknown, but it may be that they served as rest houses for travelers. They were built in ten-mile intervals along the roads. There were fifty-seven "houses of fire" on the road that connected the capitals of the Khmer Empire and Champa.

### The Temples of Jayavarman VII

Just like his Hindu predecessors, Jayavarman dedicated the second half of his reign to building temples in honor of his parents. The first one was built in 1186 and is called Ta Phom ("ancestor Brahma"). It was erected to honor the king's mother, who was depicted as Prajnaparamita, the goddess of wisdom, a central concept of Mahayana Buddhism. The temple also had a statue of Jayavarman's guru, a Buddhist teacher. This statue was surrounded by more than six hundred statues of Buddhist gods and bodhisattvas (enlightened creatures). The Buddhist temples of Jayavarman also include cells for Shaivite and Vaishnavite ascetics, right along with the dwelling cells of Buddhist monks. Ta Prohm was never restored, and it mostly lays in ruins today. It is hard to imagine what it must have looked like and what it symbolized during its glory days. Today, this temple is overgrown, with tree roots entwined around its columns, walls, and gates. It is one of the most mysterious places on Earth, and it awakens the imagination of the people.

Preah Khan ("sacred sword") was the next temple built by Jayavarman VII. The inscription of the temple mentions it was built on the site of an important battle against the Chams. Its name during the reign of Jayavarman was Jayasri ("victory and throne"), probably to symbolize the event. However, no other inscriptions mention this battle, although it is possible it was a later Cham invasion, one in which they came close to Yasodharapura but didn't manage to take it. Preah Khan was built in 1191, and it is a temple that honors Jayavarman's father, Dharanindravarman, who is depicted as Lokesvara, the deity expressing the compassion of the Buddha. The symbolism is extremely important here. In Mahayana Buddhism, wisdom and compassion united to give birth to enlightenment. Since Jayavarman's mother was depicted as wisdom and his father as the embodiment of compassion, the king was born enlightened. This trinity of wisdom, compassion, and enlightenment was central to Jayavarman's religious thinking, and these figures started popping up all around the kingdom during his reign. Even the location of the temples is symbolic. They were placed northeast and southeast of Yasodharapura's new center, Angkor Thom, which suggests that compassion and wisdom united in Yasodharapura, giving enlightenment to the land. There, in the new capital of Angkor Thom, was the Bayon Temple, which housed this enlightenment in the form of a Buddha statue.

The inscriptions on these two temples prove the magnitude of Jayavarman's kingdom, but they also show us how Cambodian bureaucracy developed, especially in terms of states' control over the duties of the population. Ta Prohm housed several thousand people, as the inscription there describes the existence of 18 high priests, 2,740 other priests, 2,232 assistants, and 12,640 people. Additionally, there were 66,625 men and women who performed services. Among them were also Burmese, Chams, and other ethnic groups who came to Cambodia. In total, there were 79,265 people around this temple. Preah Khan had a similar inscription, stating that over 100,000 people were drawn to the area from 5,300 neighboring villages. The outsiders, such as the Burmese and Chams, were accounted for differently than the Khmer population. Maybe they were prisoners or slaves gained in wars, but it is clear they had no ties to noblemen or religious institutions.

Although the temples were Buddhist, they also housed learned Hindu men and the statues of Hindu gods. Jayavarman approved of this arrangement, as he was aware that the majority of his subjects were Hindu. The temple inscriptions also mention that 13,500 villages were previously dependent on the temple sites back when they were Hindu sacred places. This means that, in total, the temple served around 300,000 people, both Buddhists and Hindu.

At the center of the new capital was the Bayon Temple. Its original name was Jayagiri ("victory mountain"), but it was renamed in the 19th century because of its obvious Buddhist imagery. The temple itself is rich with gigantic portrait imagery and bas-reliefs depicting the wars with Champa, the Indian gods, and scenes from everyday life. However, many of these were added later when the Khmer Empire reverted back to Hinduism. Primarily, the Bayon was built as a Buddhist temple. Its central statue was of Buddha shielded by a giant snake or naga. But this statue, found in the 1930s, was no longer in its original place. It was removed during the iconoclastic period after Jayavarman's death and thrown into an air shaft. Interestingly, the bas-relief scenes of the Bayon Temple depict historical scenes rather than the mythological ones taken from the *Ramayana* and *Mahabharata*. The battles that were depicted show the standard weaponry of 12$^{th}$-century Cambodia. Other segments of the reliefs show the common people buying and selling items, eating, picking fruit, taking care of children, healing the sick, traveling, and gambling, among other activities. Interestingly, these scenes, including the costumes, artifacts, and customs depicted, could be encountered in the Cambodian countryside at the end of the colonial period (Cambodia gained self-rule in 1946).

After Jayavarman's rule, Cambodian history started its period of silence. Not many inscriptions were produced, and those that were rarely even mentioned Jayavarman VII. This historical silence began during the last years of Jayavarman's reign, which might mean that he is to be blamed for it somehow. He did, after all, break the patterns of continuity evident in the rulers before him. This silence is also reflected in the sudden stop of building projects. However, maybe the inscriptions still need to be found. Only time will tell if there is more to be learned about the reign of Jayavarman VII. After him, wide-ranging social and ideological changes occurred, and they continued throughout the rest of the 13$^{th}$ century and through the 14$^{th}$ century. These changes might have been set in motion by Jayavarman himself, but it is most likely that it was his descendants' doing.

# Chapter 6 – The Crisis of the 13th Century

Angkor Wat

*Kheng Vungvuthy, CC BY-SA 4.0 <https://creativecommons.org/licenses/by-sa/4.0>, via Wikimedia Commons https://commons.wikimedia.org/wiki/File:Ankor_Wat_temple.jpg*

After the death of Jayavarman VII, Cambodia went through radical ideological changes. The throne was succeeded by Jayavarman's son, Indravarman II, but little is known about him, for his successor, Jayavarman VIII, destroyed all his inscriptions. It is believed that

Indravarman ruled in relative peace, finished the temples his father started building, and died in 1243.

The biggest change that was brought about wasn't of a royal nature but of a religious one. Jayavarman was a Mahayana Buddhist, but during his reign, Theravada Buddhism truly entered the kingdom. The presence of this sect had been in existence in Cambodia for centuries, but it was always neglected and pushed aside as a non-dominant religion. But something changed during the 13th century, as the majority of people openly converted to it. Jayavarman VIII sent one of his sons, Tamalinda, to Sri Lanka to study Theravada Buddhism and to be ordained as a monk. Tamalinda returned to Angkor and started spreading the Theravada branch of Buddhism, but it isn't likely that this mass conversion was the deed of just one man. Other wandering missionaries from Siam, Burma, and Sri Lanka also visited Angkor.

But what compelled people to suddenly change their religion? Some historians believe Theravada Buddhism was oriented toward the benefits of the common people, and because of it, the majority of the population found it easy to identify with the new religion. Others claim it was the pressure of the Mongol invasion of China that pushed the Southeast Asian nations to convert to Theravada Buddhism as it was a more militant sect. However, the most probable explanation for the sudden and fast conversion of the Khmer population could be very simple. During the expansion years of Jayavarman VII, the Khmer increased their interaction with the Mon-speaking population of northern Thailand, who were already devotees of Theravada Buddhism. Theravada Buddhism became the dominant religion, and even though it was replaced by Hinduism later, it reestablished itself. To this day, it is the official religion of Cambodia, with more than 98 percent of the citizens identifying as Theravada Buddhists.

The conversion of people in the 13th century was not total. It was fast-paced and took place on a massive scale, but it took at least half a century to establish itself as a dominant religion. When the Chinese ambassador Zhou Daguan visited Angkor in 1296, he noticed that Brahmanism and Shamanism were still very much alive, and they were also the officially approved religions next to Theravada Buddhism. But there is a huge lack of evidence regarding the 13th century in Cambodia. Possibly it was marked by a series of religious upheavals that left a certain effect on the political life of the Empire of Angkor.

The spread of Theravada Buddhism wasn't the only change that occurred in Cambodia during the 13th century. The Mongolian invasion of China shook the whole region, and a rapid and significant movement of people occurred. Foreign innovations entered the kingdom, and trade changed its well-established patterns. It is unknown if these changes were just a consequence of the general adoption of the new faith, but it is known that Brahmins, although they retained their court positions, lost their significance. With the decline of Hinduism, the bas-reliefs on the temples changed to suit Theravada Buddhism narratives. The scenes of local versions of the *Ramayana* and *Mahabharata* were replaced with images that depicted Buddhist values. Literature and iconography also changed, as well as sculptures, architecture, and the various inscriptions the kings left behind.

During the 13th century, Cambodia developed its foreign relations in two very different ways. Its grasp over the population of northern Thailand weakened, and it accepted Chinese commercial activities in Cambodian territory. Because of the Mongol expansion, China, under the early Ming dynasty, sought to expand its trade on Southeast Asian soil. However, the Chinese failed to assert their cultural influence, and the Cambodian culture remained dominant. However, Cambodian political influence over the region diminished. Some of the principalities that sent tribute to Angkor declared their independence, and to symbolize this transition, they sent tributes to the Chinese throne instead. The first to do so were Sukhothai and Louvo. In time, Laos and other principalities in the south followed their example.

Angkor became vulnerable to foreign attacks from all sides, except the east, where the weakened Champa was no longer in power. A Thai invasion occurred sometime at the end of the 13th century. The Chinese ambassador Zhou Daguan recorded it.

## Zhou Daguan in Angkor (1296–1297)

The most detailed account of life in 13th-century Cambodia was left behind by the Chinese ambassador named Zhou Daguan. He stayed in Angkor from August 1296 to sometime in 1297, during which time he wrote down his thoughts and described the appearance of Angkor. As he was not constrained by the Indian traditional belief system, he was free to describe the life of the Khmer in detail, such as bathing, trading, and marching in procession. Hindu tradition was always more concerned with the royal and divine, leaving out everyday life events. For Zhou, the Khmer were barbaric as well as exotic, and he was fascinated by their way of life. This was why he devoted his manuscript to them instead of the historical facts that we today miss. Zhou's memoirs don't reveal what happened during the years of rapid change in Cambodian society, but they do give us an insight into how the common people lived, what they did, and how they saw the world around them. Zhou's account of Cambodia is very short. Translated in English, it numbers only forty pages. It is divided into various topics, such as religion, kingship, justice, customs, slaves, vegetables, and birds, just to name a few. Incredibly, certain facets described by the Chinese envoy were still around in 20th-century Cambodia, including slavery, trial by ordeal, and sumptuary laws, though in modified form.

Five of the sections in Zhou's text deal with religion, kingship, slavery, festivals, and the king's excursions. From them, we can see that in the 13th century, Cambodia had three official religions: Brahmanism, Theravada Buddhism, and Shaivism. Zhou describes the Brahmins, saying they often occupied high offices of the court, but he couldn't say much about their religion. Zhou noticed the lack of Brahmanism schools and books from which they learned, and he never found out what was the source of their doctrine. Theravada Buddhists were more or less the same as they are today. According to Zhou, they shaved their heads, dressed in yellow robes, leaving their right shoulder exposed, and walked barefooted. He also describes Buddhist monasteries, saying that they had tile roofs, just like the houses of the high officials and the royal palace. The ordinary people had their roofs made out of thatch.

Zhou was surprised to discover that the Theravada Buddhist wats (complex of warships that included housing, temples, and schools) lacked bells, flags, cymbals, and platforms. They were much simpler than the Mahayana Buddhist temples of China. But these temples did contain a figure of Buddha, which was made out of gilded plaster. Zhou then describes the process of inscribing the sacred and historical texts on the palm leaf, a practice that survived well into the 20th century.

Zhou then describes the Shaivites. He called them "followers of the Dao" because he thought their doctrine was similar to Daoism (or Taoism). According to the Chinese ambassador, the Shaivites occupied monasteries much less prosperous than the Buddhist ones. They prayed and left offerings to no icon, and they only used a block of stone to serve as their altar. Shaivism declined after the abandonment of Angkor, and it soon disappeared, but Hindu practices and cults, including the use of lingams, continued to exist, even in modern times.

When describing the people of Angkor, Zhou noticed that many of them served in some form of slavery. People who had many slaves had more than a hundred. Those who had few slaves had anywhere between ten and twenty. The poor people, as one might expect, had no slaves. He mentioned that the slaves were usually taken from the mountain tribes. This was common in Cambodia even during the 19th century. Slaves were set apart from the rest of the people by prohibitions. They could sit and sleep only under the house, never inside. The only time a slave was allowed to enter the house was when they were performing a task. Even then, they had to kneel and bow to the floor, greeting the house and its owner before they could continue forward. The slaves had no civil privileges, and the kingdom didn't even recognize their marriages. They were forced to refer to their owners as fathers and mothers, but they were not welcomed as part of the family. The slaves constantly tried to escape, but if they were caught, they were marked by tattoos or mutilation.

Unfortunately, Zhou failed to describe the proportions of the Khmer society. We don't know if slaves or free but poor people were the majority. He rarely referred to the middle class, which existed (they owned a few slaves), or the private landowners. There were also Sino-Cambodians who were active in domestic and foreign trade. The religious figures were given special privileges, and the slaves had special prohibitions, but it remains a mystery who were the common people of the Khmer Empire. Who were the people in between, the ones without privileges or restrictions? Who were the people who made the kingdom prosper?

Next, Zhou described the celebration of New Year, which took place in November. This marked the end of the rainy season when the agricultural year started. This ceremony became known as the "Water Festival" after the 15th century when the kingdom moved the capital to Phnom Penh. Even then, it was celebrated in a similar way as described by Zhou. Big plateaus were erected from which fireworks were launched. The king and the elite families were the patrons of the celebration, and the king himself would come out to watch the fireworks. The ceremony was celebrated in Cambodia until 1970, when the monarchy was overthrown. Both the ceremony and the monarchy were reinstated in 1993.

Zhou also noticed that the Khmer had three to four rice harvests per year. However, this is very unlikely for the whole country. It was probably like that in the developed region of Angkor, where all the manpower was concentrated. The Angkor region is also known for fertile alluvial soil and for an advanced watering system, which had been perfected over several hundred years. Zhou continues to describe how Cambodia had rain for six months and then no rain for another six months. It rained every day from April until September, and during these months, the nearby Tonle Sap Lake would swell up with accumulated water. Zhou describes how, at its highest, the lake would completely cover the trees, and only their tips could be seen emerging from the water. People who lived on the banks of the lake had to move to the hills during the rainy season. The lake would dry during the months between October and March, during which time there was not a drop of rain. The boats had trouble navigating the low waters of Tonle Sap, and only the smallest and the lightest were able to cross it.

The "miracle" of Tonle Sap amazed many 19th-century travelers to Cambodia. During the dry season, the waters retreated and left behind very rich nutrients for the soil. Even after the abandonment of Angkor, the lake remained one of the most densely inhabited water surfaces in the world. Zhou was amazed by the waterworks of the Khmer Empire, but he never bothered to explain the agriculture of the land in detail. We still have many questions. How was the rice surplus handled? How much land was owned by the royal family? How much was owned by the Brahmins or Buddhist monasteries? Who were the people who cultivated the land? Were they free or slaves? But there are no answers to these questions. However, Zhou did write about Angkor markets, and astonishingly, they resemble the Cambodian markets we know today. Zhou explains that of the locals who traded, all were women. Market day was every day, and the market was open from six in the morning until noon. The products that were for sale were displayed on tumbleweed mats laid on the ground. The traders had to pay rental fees to the royal officials to use the designated mats as their selling points.

By the 13ᵗʰ century, many Chinese came to Cambodia to trade, and many of them even settled in Cambodia. Zhou describes that the products exported by Khmer were more or less the same as the ones during the Funan era. Beeswax, ivory, pepper, feathers, cardamom, and lacquer were the main items Cambodians exported until the 20ᵗʰ century. They imported ceramics, paper, metal goods, wicker, silk, and porcelain. It is unclear how the government paid for these products, but there is no evidence of Cambodians using any currency. Zhou never mentioned if Cambodians paid in kind or if they used any money.

Zhou was fascinated with the king of Angkor, Indravarman III (r. 1295–1308), and how he succeeded the throne. He said that the new king was the son-in-law of the old king, Jayavarman VIII. Upon the abdication of the old king, his daughter, Srindrabhupesvarachuda, stole her father's golden sword and presented it to her husband, thus making him a king and denying the title from Jayavarman VIII's son, her brother. The new king, according to Zhou, had a secret piece of metal sewn under his skin so that no arrow or knife could hurt him. Protected like this, he was able to leave his palace any time he wanted. Zhou wasn't in Angkor when the new king came to power, but these events were the stories he heard. Some of these events are discreetly described in inscriptions dated to the reign of Indravarman III. The Chinese ambassador also describes how the king would leave his palace. All of his soldiers would gather in front of the king, and the procession was followed by the people, who waved banners, as well as by musicians and drummers. The women of the palace would also come out, anywhere between three hundred and five hundred of them. They wore coiled-up hair-dos and were dressed in floral designs. They carried huge candles that were lit even during the day. Some women carried exotic instruments and gold and silver utensils from the palace, but their purpose is unknown, as it seems they didn't play on those instruments or eat and drink during the procession. Another contingent was made out of women who wore lances and shields. The relatives of the king, ministers, and high officials were at the front of the procession, and they rode elephants. They also carried red parasols. The king was behind them, and he would stand on his elephant. He carried a sword made out of gold in his hand, and he was shielded by twenty white parasols laced with gold.

Zhou concluded that even though Cambodia was the land of barbarians, the people knew that their ruler was supreme.

# Chapter 7 – The Abandonment of Angkor and Cambodia after the Angkorian Period

Henri Mouhot's drawing entitled Facade of Angkor Wat (1860)

*https://commons.wikimedia.org/wiki/File:Facade_of_Angkor_Wat.jpg*

Jayavarman VII was the last good king of the Khmer Empire. After his reign, the whole empire hurled into decline, eventually ending by the 15th century. Jayavarman was succeeded by Indravarman II, who, in turn, was succeeded by Jayavarman VIII. Nothing is known about Indravarman II, probably because his successor destroyed his inscriptions and statues. Jayavarman VIII (r. 1243–1295) was a Hindu king, and he was merciless toward the rising Theravada Buddhism. The Empire of Angkor was attacked by the Mongol forces, which were led by the famous Kublai Khan, during this period. It is believed that Jayavarman survived this attack because he paid the Mongols and bought peace in 1283. When Indravarman III succeeded the throne, he restored Theravada Buddhism as the state religion. A series of unremarkable kings followed, as well as more religious changes. The empire would shift from Buddhism to Hinduism, depending on the religious views of the kings who succeeded the Angkor throne. This is also the last recorded period of the Khmer Empire. It falls between Zhou's visit to Angkor and a king named Chan, who is remembered for restoring some of the old temples during the 1550s and 1560s. The centuries in between witnessed major shifts in the Angkor economy, language, foreign relations, and the structure of Cambodian society.

Inscriptions from this period are very rare. There is some evidence that comes from within the kingdom from the mid-14th century. The rest is taken from Chinese records, Cham sources, and some inscriptions from Thailand. The Thai records of the 17th century do contain some information on the political and economic conditions of the last years of the Empire of Angkor. The Cambodian chronicles, which were written much later, refer to the period but draw from folklore and the Thai chronicles. Nothing new can be learned from them. It seems that the Chinese records are the most reliable when it comes to the end of the Angkorian era. This is probably because the changes in the Cambodian political, economic, and social systems were made because of Chinese influence and their extensive trade with Southeast Asia under the Mongols and the Ming dynasty. Between 1371 and 1432, more than twenty-one embassies were sent to the Ming court, which was more than during the whole Angkorian period, probably because of the fast-developing trade between the two countries. Some of these missions were ceremonial or maybe were sent to ask China for support against common enemies. But the majority of these missions were due to trade, and the respect Cambodians received from the Chinese only testifies that Angkor was still a very influential kingdom in the region.

The Cambodian elite was now more relaxed since the old ceremonial duties of Brahmanical bureaucracy were dying out. The whole society was less rigid and probably more open to the idea of trade with neighboring kingdoms. There is no way of telling how and why this shift in Cambodian thinking and behavior occurred, but scholars believe that it wasn't the decline of the kingdom that brought about this change. Just the fact that the Cambodians were able to convince the Chinese that they were still relevant in the region speaks about the low possibilities of a sudden and catastrophic decline of Angkor. Recent studies have shown that the Angkor region was still heavily populated during the $14^{th}$ and $15^{th}$ centuries, and the local kings were able to compete for resources. Some older buildings in Angkor were even restored during the $15^{th}$ and $16^{th}$ centuries, further testifying that the region was important. There is even evidence that the occupants of the Angkor region warred with Thai peoples and with the Ayutthaya Kingdom to the west during the $17^{th}$ century. Although this was no longer the Khmer Empire, the fact that the region was inhabited at the time is evidence enough for the continuity of the kingdom.

Scholars also believe the Empire of Angkor might have gradually declined, pointing to the lack of evidence as support for their argument. There were only around one hundred inscriptions found belonging to the period between the $13^{th}$ and $15^{th}$ centuries, whereas before, there were around one thousand inscriptions made per century. This period also lacked the construction of new temples, water systems, or grandiose reservoirs. But that doesn't necessarily mean the kingdom declined. Maybe *change* and *transformation* are better terms. Cambodia continued to be a strong state, but it wouldn't have been so if the Empire of Angkor declined. But it is understandable why we are inclined to speak of decline. The kings of the period between the 14$^{th}$ and 15$^{th}$ centuries abandoned Angkor and shifted their center toward other cities, closer to the trade routes with China. However, that doesn't mean Angkor itself was completely abandoned. It continued to thrive as a city, just not as the capital city. With the royal abandonment of the city, the majority of the population moved too. Scholars argue that Angkor suddenly found itself without enough people to maintain its complex irrigation network. If they allowed the waters of the Angkor region to become stagnant, malaria-carrying mosquitos would become abundant. The population would be further depleted, which would eventually lead to the complete abandonment of the region.

Some scholars believe that the conversion to Theravada Buddhism brought changes to the nation that led to the decline of the kingdom. They used the very nature of Buddhism to explain how Angkor kings lost some territories. However, some of the neighboring people, such as the Thai and Burmese, also belonged to the Theravada Buddhism branch and were prosperous kingdoms at this time. Scholars have so far failed to connect these military victories with the pacifist nature of Buddhism. Still, many things changed within the Empire of Angkor due to the mass conversion to Theravada Buddhism. Angkorian institutions, such as inscriptions, temples, and the Hindu royal family, came to a stop or were redirected to serve a Buddhist narrative. But these social changes were not the result of religious changes exclusively. The neighboring Theravada kingdom of Ayutthaya was rising in power, so people moved there. They brought with them Angkorian ideas, texts, and traditions, and these were then modified only to be reintroduced to Cambodia in their new version. In 1431, the Thai invasion of Angkor occurred, and more people, who had been taken as war prisoners, were moved to the west. Due to the foreign invasion, the local people and the royal family moved to Phnom Penh, where they reestablished the capital of Cambodia. The capital of Cambodia is still located there today.

Phnom Penh was a suitable location for the new capital because it lies on the confluence of the Mekong and Tonle Sap. The city had existed since the 5th century CE, and it gradually developed to become a fortified city by the late 14th century. Its position was perfect for food trade operations that were flourishing with China. Cambodians would approach the Mekong Delta, which was still under Khmer control, and trade with merchants from China and Laos. Because of this, making Phnom Penh the new capital was an economic move, and as the kingdom developed its trade, it was also a logical move. The move to Phnom Penh might also have been motivated by personal or regional gains of the members of the royal family. Later, this move was legitimized, but the people left behind in Angkor were abandoned to fend for themselves in a declining empire, suffering the attacks of the neighboring kingdoms. To legitimize the move of the capital from Angkor to Phnom Penh, a myth of the city's foundation was developed. A lady named Penh found a floating tree in the waters of Tonle Sap. She pulled it out on the shore and found four figures of Buddha and one of Vishnu inside of the tree. This was a symbol that the area was blessed and that it would prosper under the patronage of both Buddhist and Hindu deities.

The new capital's importance to trade is mirrored in the abundant presence of foreigners. Phnom Penh housed Malay speakers from Champa and the islands of Indonesia. They influenced the Khmer language and left behind words such as *kompong* ("landing place") and *psar* ("market"). The Malay legacy in Cambodia still needs to be researched, for it seems that it runs deeper. The descriptions of 17th-century Cambodian political systems strongly resemble the one that existed in riverine Malaya at the time. Other foreigners who left their mark on the new capital were the Chinese. In the 1540s, there were three thousand Chinese living in Phnom Penh, and they started intermarrying into the Cambodian elite families.

The previous social organization, bureaucracy, and economic priorities of Angkor heavily depended on slavery and forced labor. However, by the end of the 15th century, these were no longer relevant. Nor was the heavy taxation of the people and their divide into the castes. New forms of social organization entered the kingdom, along with new patterns of settlements and new economic priorities. This was all due to the connections Cambodia developed with its neighbors through trade. The change was on a much larger scale than just the Empire of Angkor. It happened in the whole of Southeast Asia, and by the end of the 16th century, the Empire of Angkor and the rising Ayutthaya Kingdom regarded each other not as separate polities but as common participants in one hybrid culture. This hybrid culture was a mixture of Hinduinized kingship and Theravada principles of monarchy. The old Angkorian ideology met the new Theravada to form a unique civilization. But they also included the remnants of paternalistic village-oriented leadership of the Thai people and tribal peoples of the hills of southern China. The Khmer language was an official language in both kingdoms during the 14th century, and they shared a common religion as well, which was also accessible to ordinary people too. These people came in contact with each other through war, trade, immigration, and their shared religion, and together, they developed a separate cultural tradition, abandoning the old, completely Hinduinized way of life.

### Cambodia in the 15th and 16th Centuries

Little is known about the events in the Angkor region immediately after the Thai invasion. It seems that the Thai administration was overthrown by the forces of Phnom Penh sometime in the middle of the 15th century. It is believed that the names of the kings who ruled from Phnom Penh during this period are all fictional, even though they are recorded in local chronicles. However, we know that at the end of the 15$^{th}$ century, a new conflict arose between the local rulers. One of these rulers became the dominant one. Some sources claim he was a former slave, while the European writings of the 19$^{th}$ century claim he was a relative of a former monarch. Nevertheless, he exiled the former king, Chan I, who found refuge in Ayutthaya. But Chan returned to power later and brought with him a Thai army that helped him depose the usurper. Chan's restoration to power under Thai patronage was seen as a bad omen, and the eastern provinces, from where the usurper hailed, remained rebellious. From the 1620s onward, they often sought help from their Vietnamese neighbors.

A Cambodian chronicle mentions that a Khmer king married a Vietnamese princess in the 1630s and allowed the Vietnamese people to establish a base in the Mekong Delta. By that time, the Mekong Delta was still predominantly inhabited by the Khmer but was outside of Cambodia's direct control. The next two hundred years saw Vietnamese immigrants pouring into the region and taking full administrative control over it. Even today, Cambodians call this region Lower Cambodia or Kampuchea Krom, and the Khmer people are a significant part of the Vietnamese culture that developed in the region. The Thai presence in the north and the Vietnamese presence to the east created a competitive atmosphere for dominance over the Cambodian court. The people were divided into those who supported the Thai and those who supported the Vietnamese. This factionalism was already very severe in the 1680s, and it stayed like this until the 1860s.

The first European who mentioned Cambodia in his writings was probably Tomé Pires, a Portuguese apothecary. He joined one of the first European expeditions to Southeast Asia, and he wrote *Suma Oriental*, a book on Asian trade. He described the Cambodian kingdom as a warlike one, with a superior ruler who obeyed no one. But Pires was relying on hearsay when he hinted about the riches that could be gained from Cambodia. He never really visited the state but rather collected the stories from merchants and mariners in the ports of India and China. The first European who was an eyewitness to 16<sup>th</sup>-century Cambodia was a Portuguese missionary named Gaspar da Cruz. He visited Longvek during the reign of King Chan I in 1556. He spent only one year there, as he was unable to convert the Khmer to Christianity. He blamed the strong influence of Buddhism and the superstition of the Khmer people. However, he did describe the loyalty of the Cambodian people to their king. According to Cruz, the people dared do nothing without the king's approval, and they were unable to make complicated decisions without their ruler. Cruz also described how more than a third of able-bodied Cambodians were part of the *sangha,* a Buddhist community of monks and nuns. He also mentioned that the rest of the population was loyal to the Buddhist monks and even regarded them as living gods.

Cruz was also astonished by the organization of Cambodian society and the role of the king. According to him, if a man of the house died, all his possessions were returned to the king, while his wife and children went off to find a better future somewhere else. They did steal what they could, though. This means that people held possessions only at the king's pleasure, and this went for ranks, land, and social positions as well. This demonstrates that the kingship in the 16<sup>th</sup> century retained the absolutism of the Angkorian model, even after the mass conversion to Buddhism. Due to this absolutism, the elite families could not unite into opposition to the king, as the king would easily dispose of them. Cruz never mentioned Angkor, and it is possible he never even knew of its existence or importance.

# Conclusion

In 1599, Portuguese writer Diego do Couto visited Cambodia, and he wrote down the stories he heard. One of them described an event that happened some forty years before his arrival to Cambodia (around 1550). The king was on the hunt when he stumbled upon some ruins. He was amazed by the height of the walls he saw, and he ordered his people to cut the vines and branches that were obstructing the entrance to the ruins. Thousands of people worked for several days so that the king could go inside and marvel at the construction of his ancestors. Once he got inside, he was awed by the beauty and craftsmanship of the place and decided to move his court to the ruins and rebuild the whole site. These ruins were the remnants of Angkor, left behind and forgotten by its people. There are no other sources that describe this event, but there are several inscriptions in Angkor dated to the 1560s, which would approximately correspond to the date of its rediscovery. But it is more likely that Angkor was rediscovered during a military campaign, as Cambodia was at war with Siam at the time. The Angkor region was a logical place to station the Cambodian army if an invasion of Siam was planned.

But even though Angkor was once again the capital city of the Khmer, it quickly fell out of use, and the people returned to Phnom Penh. The ruins of Angkor Wat were again discovered in 1860 by a

French naturalist named Henri Mouhot. His writings were published three years later, posthumously since he died in Cambodia in 1861. In them, Mouhot described his visit to Angkor and the awe he felt when he first saw the ruins of Angkor Wat. He described how he wondered about the greatness of the past Khmer civilization, which was now, according to him, a barbaric nation. In his native France, the publication was received with awe, and Mouhot was credited with the "discovery of the lost city of Angkor." However, the excitement about this discovery is somewhat controversial as the city was never really lost. The locals knew exactly where it was, and they were aware of its past importance. Mouhot was not even the first foreigner to visit the site. Before him, during the 16$^{th}$ and 17$^{th}$ centuries, Portuguese and Spanish explorers described Angkor and their visits. In the 17$^{th}$ century, the site was even inhabited, mostly by Japanese, who left their inscriptions on the pillars of the city. When Mouhot visited Angkor Wat, there was a settlement on its site, and the place was abundant with life. The better phrasing would be that in 1860, the Western world rediscovered Angkor Wat. And ever since then, the Westerners' interests in Angkor have never ceased.

The same year the writings of Henri Mouhot were published, Cambodia became the protectorate of France. Interest in this new and exotic country only grew. In 1898, the French School of the Far East (EFEO) was founded with the task of studying Cambodia's past, archaeology, art, and language. Thanks to this school, many more ruins in Cambodia were discovered, especially once the usage of LiDAR in archaeology started. Angkor, even though it was still inhabited, was overgrown, and it was damaged by wars and earthquakes. In the early 1900s, the French dedicated much of their funds to the restoration of Angkor Wat and its opening to its first visitors. Since those early days, tourists have been coming to see one of the largest ancient temples on Earth. Mesmerized by its decorations, elaborate bas-reliefs, and statues, many compare it to the works of Renaissance artists. The temple became a UNESCO World

Heritage Site in 1992, and it is still a very spiritual place for the Buddhist monks and their followers. For the rest of the world, Angkor is a mysterious and magical place, and its popularity only continues to grow.

Here's another book by Captivating History that you might like

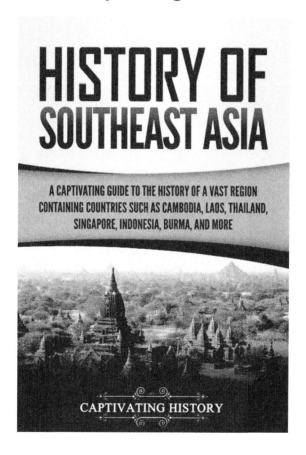

# Free Bonus from Captivating History (Available for a Limited time)

Hi History Lovers!

Now you have a chance to join our exclusive history list so you can get your first history ebook for free as well as discounts and a potential to get more history books for free! Simply visit the link below to join.

Captivatinghistory.com/ebook

Also, make sure to follow us on Facebook, Twitter and Youtube by searching for Captivating History.

# References

Cambodia - The Khmer state (Angkor). (n.d.). Encyclopedia Britannica.

https://www.britannica.com/place/Cambodia/The-Khmer-state-Angkor

Chandler, D. (2007). *A History of Cambodia, 4th Edition (4th ed.)*. Routledge.

Khmer Empire | Encyclopedia.com. (n.d.). Encyclopedia.

https://www.encyclopedia.com/history/encyclopedias-almanacs-transcripts-and-maps/khmer-empire

Ortner, J., Mabbett, I. W., Goodman, J., Mabbett, I., Mannikka, E., & Sanday, J. (2002).

*Angkor: Celestial Temples of the Khmer (1st ed.)*. Abbeville Press.

Plubins, R. Q. (2021, March 17). Khmer Empire. World History Encyclopedia.

https://www.ancient.eu/Khmer_Empire/

So, K. T., & So, J. (2017a). *The Khmer Kings and the History of Cambodia: BOOK I –*

*1st Century to 1595: Funan, Chenla, Angkor and Longvek Periods.* DatASIA, Inc.

So, K. T., & So, J. (2017b). *The Khmer Kings and the History of Cambodia: BOOK I - 1st Century to 1595: Funan, Chenla, Angkor and Longvek Periods.* DatASIA, Inc.

Printed in Great Britain
by Amazon

37760025R00056